Why CATS
are
ASSHOLES

Why CATS are ASSHOLES

LIZ MIELE

ILLUSTRATED BY CHELSEA TROUSDALE

Skyhorse Publishing

Skyhorse Publishing books may be purchased in bulk at special discounts for sales promotion, corporate gifts, fund-raising, or educational purposes. Special editions can also be created to specifications. For details, contact the Special Sales Department, Skyhorse Publishing, 307 West 36th Street, 11th Floor, New York, NY 10018 or info@skyhorsepublishing.com.

Skyhorse® and Skyhorse Publishing® are registered trademarks of Skyhorse Publishing, Inc.®, a Delaware corporation.

Visit our website at www.skyhorsepublishing.com.

10 9 8 7 6 5 4

Library of Congress Cataloging-in-Publication Data is available on file.

Cover design by Chelsea Trousdale and Brian Peterson
Cover illustrations credit: Chelsea Trousdale

ISBN: 978-1-5107-5622-9
Ebook ISBN: 978-1-5107-5623-6

Printed in China

To my parents and my cat, Pasta.
All three taught me everything I know.

CONTENTS

INTRODUCTION

Hi! I'm a stand-up comedian and have been writing and telling jokes half my life. Whenever someone asks me what's my act like, what's my schtick, I always tell them, "I mostly tell cat jokes." They always follow up with, "Is there a demand for that?" and the answer is, "No . . . not really," I think because most cat people are introverted homebodies that can't bother to put on non-comfy pants to go to a comedy club. (I get it, I'm with you!) I *am* also on YouTube and Spotify, but just go along with this theory . . .

So I thought, why not continue my underground punk band–like legacy and expand my cat jokes to a cat book, taking a deep dive into the complexity of our love for felines. Are they tiny adorable terrorists that don't love us? OR are they tiny adorable terrorist that *do* love us? Let me help you solve this mystery once and for all!

But first, let me be honest and open. I have a degree in nothing. In fact, I can barely read. Enjoy what I've written, but please don't take it seriously. It's not up for debate. This isn't Twitter. I'm not trying to sway or shame anyone. Cat shaming will not be tolerated! This is merely a passion project to be enjoyed by the millions of cat lovers that just get it.

Why Cats are Assholes

A bit of background. Both my parents are veterinarians. They're educated in the field, but I'm just a cat lover with more free time than you.

I have a cat named Pasta, who is both the love of my life and simultaneously the worst thing that has ever happened to my favorite things. (RIP my favorite purse, backpack, half my shoes, and the right side of my comforter.) I think that's what real love is, being able to see all their flaws and loving them for who they are. Never really knowing if my cat loves me back is what keeps our relationship fresh and fun. Is she coming over to cuddle, or bite me? After fifteen years I still don't know. I think that's all you need to know to enjoy this book. Yes, you can love something so much you take pictures of it every day and show strangers on the subway, but also question why you allow it walk on your face while you sleep. You can't change them, and this book is here to help you understand why.

I have a lot of theories. I think about this stuff all the time. People ask about our ethnic background as a way to not just identify us but to "understand our behavior." It's weird. I don't know how my grandfather being Italian makes you understand why I'm yelling in this deli . . . oh wait, now I get it. But maybe, understanding your cats' rote behaviors will help you get them better. Perhaps bring you closer or make you realize that ferrets aren't that bad. I dunno. This book is neither a positive nor negative look at cats. It's just one woman asking one species, *Why do you always cry at 3 a.m.?*

Thanks for reading! And I'll say this: if at any time you feel the need to show me how cute or weird or crazy your cat is, I fully welcome all unsolicited cat pictures! They are the only

reason I go on social media. Tag me on IG or Twitter **@lizmiele** and **#WhyCatsAreAssholes**.

MEET PASTA

I had a few cats growing up: Max (technically my older sister's cat) was black and white; Sancho, who died very young (also black and white); and all the cats that lived at my mom's clinic next door. But Pasta was *my* first cat. I was nineteen and I

had just moved into my first apartment in New York City. And because I had been living in dorms, I had gone two full years without living with a pet—which I had never experienced and didn't enjoy. I desperately needed a companion to ignore me, so I told my mom and she began scouting for some prospects. Every time she had a client come in with a pregnant cat or with kittens, she'd snoop. "Do these need a home?" But no luck.

Then Ashley, one of my best friends from high school, had a cat on her farm that had kittens and I jumped on a train back to New Jersey to find me a kitty buddy. The litter was one grey tabby (my favorite color/pattern, if I'm being honest, but it was already spoken for) and six all-black cats. So I sat on the ground playing with all of the kittens to find my new best friend. Pasta was so sweet and playful and cuddly! I loved her from the start and took her home immediately.

And she was never like that again.

Barely joking . . . but I did feel tricked. She was bitey, scratchy, uncuddly, and distant for probably a little over three years. I wanted a friend and instead got a Craigslist roommate. She sucked for a long time, and as this was my first cat I felt like I'd fucked up. Like I made a bad choice or, worse, that I was a bad cat mom. Either way, I stuck with her. It felt the same way a real mom doesn't have a choice when her kids suck. (Does this mean I'm ready to be a mom? Oh man!)

When I'd go out of town for shows I'd drop her off at my mom's clinic and she'd have to be in a cage away from all the other cats with notes that read "Watch out she swipes!" or "Not friendly!" or "Filled with murderous rage. Will try to lure you in with her cuteness then tricks you and tries to scratch your eyes out. Don't trust. Bring back up." Heartbreaking! We are Italian! The only redeeming quality we have is that we are friendly. "WHO HURT YOU?! You are making us look bad, Pasta!" Every time she got a bad report card when I picked her up, I felt shame. I'd say those cliché client things like, "She's not like this at home." But it was kinda a lie. She wasn't as angry, but she had a lot of emotional baggage for a kitten.

We had our good and bad moments, and a little after three years she stopped being so angry at the world, and softened more each year. She cuddled more and soon became like a helicopter cat. She'd greet me at the door, follow me from room to room, watch me shower, sit on my lap when I was on the toilet, crawl in my lap the moment I sat anywhere, watch me cook, wanted to be held like a child (tall roommates and boyfriends were her fav, and they would carry her around the apartment doing errands. She loved it!), and when she wasn't following me around she was sitting somewhere high guarding the place, or deep in a closet taking a nap. Now when I drop her off at the cat clinic, she is beloved. Older staff would tell tales of what a terror she was and newer staff would hold her and say, "I can't believe it! Not this cuddly angel!" She no longer hates other cats and even has cat friends, roaming free at the practice and welcoming everyone like an ambassador or Walmart greeter. Some kitties need extra love and time. I'll be bringing her up a lot in this book, so just wanted you to know her story. She's like the beast from *Beauty and the Beast*, but she's been cute the whole time!

Quick Pasta Breakdown

The same way I know my boyfriend and best human friends, I know my cat. I think it's important to acknowledge that, yes, all

Why Cats are Assholes

cats have similarities but are also unique snowflakes with their own personalities and wounds, and you should know their likes, dislikes, and what they are indifferent about. They are essentially your roommate. If you don't wanna always be yelling at them for doing wind sprints at 3 a.m., it might help to know why they are doing it in the first place and find a solution or compromise. I'll talk later on how to gather some of this information and truly get to know your cat.

But here are Pasta's likes, dislikes, and what she tolerates, collected over fifteen years of cohabitation. It was interesting to sit and list them all out at once and realize how well I do know her. Might be a nice exercise for you and something you can add to and give to sitters. Like:

"Don't eat ice cream around her unless you wanna share. She likes to watch people shower, so just let her and she likes to pick out her own PJs. I'll be back in four days!"

Name: Pasta
Birthday: May 2, 2005
Likes:
- Being held by tall people (I'm 5-foot-1)
- Napping under blankets or in dark spaces, like deep in the closet (will sleep on shoes, does not care)
- Sitting on anything I'm working on or in front of anything I'm looking at or touching (phone, computer, TV, books, notebooks, make-up)
- Meat in any form, ice cream (goes fucking nuts . . . cannot eat it around her. She has a problem), and olive oil (will lick it off my food or hands . . . it's weird. She's so Italian!)

- Playing with mice and bugs, but not fully killing them . . . just ruining their day and injuring them (also feels like a mafia Italian move)
- Knocking over anything sentimental and irreplaceable
- Biting feet while dead asleep
- Head and neck scratches
- Being brushed (back, tail, and head only)
- Watching TV together

Dislikes:

- Belly rubs, touching her paws
- Me moving when she is napping
- Passively petting without paying attention
- Me being awake but not paying attention to her
- Cats that don't respect her age and authority
- Cages or carriers of any kind
- Any kind of transit in said carrier
- Being moved without asking
- Not being fed immediately when I come home or she asks
- Being locked out of rooms (including bathrooms, closets, and the great outdoors)

Things She Tolerates:

- Being dressed up (She was an actress in my web series *Apt C3* for years! Dressed her up a lot! Such a pro!)
- Being held by short people
- Sleeping *not* on top of me

xv

- Automatic toys
- Hanging with other cats
- Pulling back her ears so she looks like she got a furlift. Doesn't love or hate, but she's let me and my roommates do it for years and I am grateful. She looks so funny. I can't stop.

FREQUENTLY ASKED CAT QUESTION

Question: How do I let my cat know that it's an asshole?

Answer: Sometimes it's hard to sit your cat down and explain how their behavior affects you. I'd start by placing this book next to their litter box or bed. I'm not against passive aggressively suggesting that your cat get its life together. If your cat isn't a big reader, maybe read it to them!

1

A BRIEF HISTORY ON WHY CATS ARE ASSHOLES

In today's society, black cats continue to be seen as bad luck and have trouble getting adopted. Parents with newborns are scared to have cats around their babies, and people in general have no problem voicing that they hate cats. But before they were cast aside with bad raps, they lived a semi-charmed life as gods and good luck charms in many cultures.

ANCIENT EGYPT: WE BELIEVE CATS ARE GODS

Cats! Humans' first best friend before the dog PR came in and started their smear campaign. "They don't love you," "They mostly just sleep on your stuff," "They will eat you before your body is cold." I mean, these are all kinda true. But why can't we appreciate how resilient and well rested these animals are and stop judging them cause they aren't literal gullible lap dogs? I 100 percent get the loyalty people have toward their dogs. They greet you when you come home, they are cuddly, they listen, they do tricks, their bathroom is outside and doesn't stink up the house, they seem to care about you and your well-being. But what if you didn't grow up with love and affection?

Why Cats are Assholes

What if you like chasing attention, questioning if your cat is deaf, dumb, or just indifferent to you and/or their name? What if you like being bit cause it reminds you that you're alive? Some of us out here like to earn our love or it isn't real! But this book isn't about shitting on dogs. It's mostly about shitting on cats. We love them, but why?

It's believed that the Ancient Egyptians domesticated cats over 4,000 years ago. Egyptians thought cats were magical creatures that could bring good luck to any home that had one. They worshipped them for their hunting skills, ability to control the pest population, and because they are so damn cute!

And they are still utilized for these skills (read: cuteness) today. Everyone talks about seeing-eye dogs, bomb- or drug-sniffing dogs, emotional support dogs, how dogs protect and rescue owners . . . but cats? Cats are the reason your cereal hasn't been tested by mice first! They are on the front lines, protecting you against the spread of disease! They were on ships, in stores, in homes. All to keep us safe from tiny intruders (rodents) who harbored microscopic intruders (disease). Yeah, dogs protect against murderers in the night, but cats protect against disease murder (or something, I'm not a scientist). Point being: they *are* useful, even if listening isn't their strong suit. They are like teenage boys. Yes, they leave the bathroom a disaster, but when they mow the lawn or drive their sister to soccer practice you remember why you had them.

If Ancient Egypt Had the Internet, It Would Be Illegal to Give a Cat Video a Thumbs Down

The Ancient Egyptians saw their usefulness and didn't just like them and make an Instagram account for them or develop a sock line with their face on it. They worshipped them. They made temples in their honor. It was a crime to kill them. I feel like we've lost touch with this. Did you know Australia is trying to exterminate *all* stray cats? Supposedly it is because they are hurting the wild bird population. How is this not a recipe for trouble when they wipe out cats and start to realize all the unseen good they do? Like how we hate bees but the earth would crumble if they went extinct (more on this later). Moral of the story: cats are important, and their viral videos are what hold the Internet together!

3

Why Cats are Assholes

When I was a little girl, I was obsessed with Egypt for this history of cat worship alone. I felt like maybe ethnicity shouldn't be about heritage and DNA but more what culture your soul connects with. I love baklava and cats and quite frankly look middle eastern. I think that should be enough to at least become an honorary Egyptian. (Don't stress, I'm not gonna culturally appropriate anyone. I just have a necklace with my name spelled in hieroglyphics and an obscene amount of cat trinkets.) But my best friend is Egyptian (coincidence?), so can she deem it so? Most women already do their make-up like Cleopatra. Cat eye eyeliner was before its time! Cat love was before its time. I feel like only now and only because of the Internet has cat worship been even close to those of the Egyptians. Don't get me wrong, I'm not gonna kill my cat so we can go to the afterlife together. But is it too much to ask that she want that? And if that's what she wanted, I wouldn't fight her. Do you see the difference? It's about choice. It's about autonomy. It's about a cat's choice to die with its owners or continue to live among their stuff and become the king/queen of the household they always acted like they were.

Things the Egyptians Did for Cats

Egyptians had a lot of intense cat love traditions. Some made me think they all had *Toxoplasmosis* (the parasite that makes humans love cats), but some felt right and I believe that we should consider bringing a few of them back. Here are a handful that were customary and my feelings on whether we should or shouldn't get back to our kitty worship roots.

4

1. **Dressed Cats in Jewels and Fed Them Fancy Treats**

   I mean, who's not doing that now? With how fun collars are and how expensive kitty treats have become, this feels like it never stopped. People are feeding their cats organic cat food when I can't even afford organic human food! Honestly, replace jewels with cat hats and fancy treats with meat I drop on the floor and, really, I've been treating my cat like a queen since day one! So my answer is yes, let's do this/keep doing this. I actually think I have some earrings that would look amazing on Pasta. Queen, P!

2. **Mummified Cats and Buried Them in Their Own Cemetery**

   OK. If I wasn't an environmentalist and also extremely lazy, I'd be down for bringing this back. Cause one: *who doesn't wanna be haunted by future cat mummies*; and two: cat's love hanging out in boxes. This feels like the ultimate afterlife gift. "Here's a nicer box for you to be buried in!" You can bury them with their favorite toys. Maybe with the kid you like the least. Maybe, instead of a traditional graveyard, it's like a sandbox. They call it "the eternal litter box." Instead of leaving flowers on their grave you'd leave cans of tuna. Dude, the more I think about it, the more I wanna start this . . . but I'm not going to. We don't have the space for human bodies, it's bad for the environment, it's expensive, and I honestly think burial of humans is silly. I'm pro cremation (turning your cat into litter . . . too much?) and putting them in a nice box. A box they would have loved if alive.

3. **Owners Shaved Off Their Eyebrows and Mourned Their Cat's Death Until They Grew Back**

   What is this, the '90s? No, I'm sorry. Just no. I love my eyebrows. It's the only thing I religiously upkeep (cause it costs $6!) and it makes a face. We all know that. Also, women pretty much shave most things off for society. I'm not giving up the last bit of my adult hair for my cat. Sorry kitties. Also, why eyebrows? That's such a weird way to show you are sad. Also not having eyebrows means people have no idea how you feel. Maybe we can amend this one. Like, to mourn a cat we get a tiny tattoo. I mean, I already want a tiny cat tattoo. Plus I do love the idea of having a pet graveyard of sorts on my body. It would be the truest definition of a cat lady. "She had eighteen cat tattoos, she is such an authentic cat lady." I'd do that. Or sit in a cardboard box every day for an hour. All realistic, thoughtful ways to show sadness and respect, and no one has to look like Whoopi Goldberg in the process.

4. **Cat Art**

   This has never stopped and, in fact, I'm a big collector of it. I have such a hard time resisting all forms of cat art. When I was a kid, I'd cut up old *Cat Fancy* magazines and glue my favorite cat pictures into my own notebook (don't ask). My parents would always buy me cat calendars, and when the year was over I'd cut out the cats I liked best (which was usually all of them) and tape them to my wall. I mean, my room was pretty dope in elementary school. And these behaviors have almost barely changed. My walls are littered with cat art (all

6

art, but lots of cats depicted) stickers, postcards, paintings, prints, you name it. I follow so many artists that paint cats on Instagram. I own numerous amounts of cat shirts, sweatshirts, and pairs of socks. I have cat figurines, and trinkets I've been collecting since I was a kid, and my boyfriend just bought me a cat teapot! I love it. My room looks like a runaway teenager from Japan and I don't care. I like them. They make me happy. I'm hurting no one. No, you're weird!

5. If a Cat Was Killed—Even by Accident—the Killer Was Sentenced to Death

This is a resounding yes. From reading horrific articles about teenagers throwing cats in bags off bridges to kill shelters still existing, a life for a life seems fair to me. Or, let's make it an online vote. Let's *America's Got Talent* it, but with lives. They tell America what they did to the cat and we vote if they deserve to live or die. If this is too drastic, maybe we just don't let them have access to the Internet—something as harsh as murder in today's society. If killing animals is an early sign of a serial killer, is this not a preventive measure to saving human lives?

JAPAN: A GIANT CAT CAFÉ OF A COUNTRY

I went on vacation to Japan a year ago, a dream of mine since as long as I can remember. I don't know if I did the same little kid research about Japan that I did with Egypt, but I just always knew they were as cat obsessed as I was. But nothing prepared me for how cat crazy they were until I got there. It was like a cat café of a country. Cartoon cats advertised everything from restaurants to toys, clubs to temples. Ads for cat cafés seemed to be on every block, stores littered with cat paraphernalia. I was in heaven. I felt understood. And yes, I bought a lot of stickers.

Most people recognize Maneki-neko (which roughly translates to "beckoning cat"), which is the cat figurine with a paw raised, sometimes moving forward and back, because they are in the window of most Japanese and even Chinese restaurants. Originally appearing in the 1800s, it is supposed to bring good luck to shops and businesses.

It comes from a popular Japanese folklore that involves a down-on-his-luck store owner who, despite being close to going out of business, takes in a stray cat. After eating, the cat sat outside the business and beckoned customers to come in and shop (hence the idea of the moving paw). Because of this folklore, cats represent good fortune and prosperity in business, which is called *fuku neko*, meaning "lucky cat." They are beloved and respected . . . as they should be.

This folklore pretty much came true in modern Japan, when a failing train station decided to rejuvenate their station by making a stray cat that hung around the new station master and operating officer. Tama, the station master cat at Kishi Station on the Kishigawa Line in Kinokawa, Wakayama Prefecture, Japan, is now a major tourist attraction! In the late '90s, Tama used to hang around the station, and passengers affectionately called her the station master. She was taken care of by a local convenience store owner, who asked the new president of the station to take care of her years later when he was leaving the area. The president of the company was a dog person but fell for Tama—hard. Soon after adopting the stray cat, Kojima ordered a customized stationmaster hat for the kitty and, in 2007,

A Brief History on Why Cats Are Assholes

he officially named Tama "Stationmaster of Kishi Station"—the first feline stationmaster in Japan. Her duties were to be the face of the railway and appear in promotional material and media coverage and greet passengers. She was so beloved that a commissioned portrait was painted of her, which hangs in the station's souvenir shop. She was promoted to "Super Station manager" in 2008, and this began to draw more tourists to the station. According to a 2008 study, the number of passengers on the Kishigawa line has increased by almost 300,000 from 2006! It helped the railway so much that, in 2010, they hired an award-winning industrial designer to redesign the exterior and interior as a completely Tama-themed line.

I love this story so much. First of all, it's the best underdog (undercat!) story of a stray cat being seen for its heart, changing people's lives for the better, and never being broke and living on the streets again. It's like *Aladdin*, but if he was the prince all along! Why hasn't Disney turned this into a movie yet, and if they do PLEASE LET ME VOICE THE CAT!

We talk about cats having value because they kill rodents and pests, but here a cat changed a business just because she wore a dope hat. We need to start seeing the simple beauty of just having cats around. Whenever I see a failing business now I think *You know what you need? A cat greeter! A cat manager! A cat CEO!* Yes, they might bite a customer or two, but maybe they were gonna steal or something. You don't know. As this has proven, cats save businesses!

But my favorite thing that I saw while visiting Japan was in Kyoto. I was walking around this kinda hallway of small shops. There was food, arcades, and little shops—one of which was filled with small handmade magnets of cats wearing clothes

9

and doing activities. Most of them either had a music or ghost theme. All the magnets were handmade by a sweet old man, and the cat on most of them were inspired by his cat. The shop was called Swing Masa Jazz House. He's been written up a bunch (you can Google him), but if you are reading this book I have zero doubt this will become your favorite place on earth. It's a workspace, shop, and museum filled top to bottom with handmade cat magnets. He made me feel welcome, served me green tea, and let me browse his shop for as long as my heart needed. My boyfriend abandoned me there and I looked through all the art for over an hour. I now own two of his pieces! And I was so cat crazy in Japan we almost broke up. (Not sure if that is true, but he did not prepare for how happy Japan was going to make me and how often I would just wander off to follow a cat.)

MODERN AMERICA: I CAN SEE HOW CATS WERE RAISED TO BELIEVE THEY WERE GODS

You know that kid that was told they were perfect and a gift from God every day and then grows up to be talentless and obnoxious . . . well, that's cats. They are 100 percent a product of blind worship that has gone to their heads and now resonates in their DNA forever. We told them they were gods thousands of years ago and they took it to heart.

In their defense, I get one YouTube comment that says, "You're funny" and I walk around with big-dick energy for three weeks. But I often feel like cats walk around like a teacher that has tenure. They don't care about the job anymore and they know they can't get fired so they just do whatever the fuck they feel like in the moment and with an arrogance and nonchalance of a narcissist that can't feel others' pain. (That's right. I'm talking about you, Mr. Miller!) I feel like a lot of their behavior can be traced back to being treated like royalty in the past. Knocking things over that are in their way. Total "my dad's a billionaire" behavior. Biting you when you don't pet them or give them the attention they feel they deserve. That comes from an ancestry of having servants. Hiding when others come over cause you don't wanna say hi. That would never have been acceptable in my house growing up. What the Japanese and Egyptians don't know is they accidently helped raise spoiled brats and, thousands of years later, we are justifying it.

Everyone: "Cats are assholes"
Cat Lovers: "No, they are just accustomed to a certain way of life. You don't get it!"

American Cat Myths All Seem to Be Negative

It seems like modern America is split down the middle on how we feel about cats. There are the ones that put up with their bad behavior because they are too cute to hate, and there are the people that never met or spent time with a cat and just go with the bad press—and the press is BAD. Rumors, myths, and folklore all point to cats being the reason why your life sucks. I'll never understand superstitious people; it's as silly as horoscopes and fortune cookies. Yes, they are a fun distraction. But do what I do: believe the positive and call them dumb if they are negative. It's been working for me for years! Be cat avoidant if you are allergic, but don't be cat avoidant cause you heard a rumor from the 1800s—they didn't even have science then! If you don't take medical advice from those old doctors, why are

you listening to their cat facts, too? Let's debunk this junk once and for all.

Black Cats = Bad Luck
The origin of this myth is uncertain, but people think it may have to do with a cat's stealthy nature. Cats in general see better in the dark, black cats tend to blend in with the night, and cats themselves are known to be sneaky—especially when hunting prey or are scared. I can't tell you how many times my cat has attacked my feet out of nowhere. It would be quite impressive if I wasn't so busy being angry.

Most of Europe associates black cats with bad luck—especially if one walks in front of you. It was believed to be an omen of misfortune and death. Cool bro, but how? Because they are dark? Take responsibility for not washing your hands and/or being a bad person. Don't put that on cats. They're just trying to get somewhere.

This myth has always pissed me off because it's most definitely the reason black cats get adopted less today. Pasta is all black with gold eyes, and while she wasn't my first choice (covered earlier) she presented her case and I chose her. She has brought love, joy, anger, frustration, and vomit into my life, and I will forever be grateful for learning how to deal with these mixed emotions and bodily fluids. Cats are cats. Don't judge them by the color of their fur but by the content of their character. I don't know who said that, but it's profound and they should definitely have a holiday.

But that's not the only reason black cats aren't trusted. In Ancient Greece, according to Greek mythology, Zeus's wife Hera once transformed her servant, Galinthias, into a black cat as punishment for impeding the birth of Hercules. Galinthias went on to become an assistant to Hecate, the goddess of witchcraft, and black cats have had associations with bad luck and witchcraft ever since. So we hate cats because of a story? This seems childish. It would be like if you hated candy because of Hansel and Gretel. Not everyone who owns a candy shop is trying to eat you! (That being said, don't trust any adult luring you with candy . . . maybe this was a bad example.) Anyway, shit's not real! We have Google now. Fact check your beliefs.

Europeans, and later, early settlers in America, thought black cats assisted witches in their evil deeds, and also that witches could transform into black cats to lurk in the shadows and perform magic spells on people. Both witches and black cats were persecuted and killed together. My first thought reading that is, "Jesus, that's horrific." Second thought is "aww best friends forever!"

It was also believed that a witch could shapeshift into a black cat up to nine times, which may have something to do with the belief that cats have nine lives. In today's movies, cartoons, and during Halloween, black cats are often featured either as witches or alongside witches. I can see how we are perpetuating the myth, but that's actually one of the reasons I loved Halloween because every decoration looked like my cat (plus the free candy!).

But by continuing to tell kids black cats are to be feared creates a new generation of black-cat shunners. It also has negative effects toward women who live alone that love arts and crafts and own cats . . . which is pretty much who I am. Just replace spells with making things with glitter and I'm essentially a modern-day sorceress. I don't even think witches would survive today. Now if you need a weird ingredient to break a curse you can just get it off Amazon. All this said, witches (read: independent women with knowledge, a.k.a. feminists, a.k.a. all women in 2020) and black cats are just friends. Let's stop projecting weird stuff on top them, shall we?

Here are a few things I love about owning a black cat:

- She often looks like Batman
- She blends into dark spaces so much so that when she opens her eyes it just looks like my closet has floating eyes like cartoons
- Her fur doesn't show up on my clothes (I wear a lot of black . . . oh wait, am I a witch?)
- All hats and clothing I put on her really pop!
- She looks very slim all the time
- She's always Halloween ready!

Cats Have Nine Lives
The origins of cats having nine lives is unknown, but there are many theories. The myth that they have multiple lives exists in a lot of different cultures, but the numbers vary. It's seven in parts of Spain, while in Turkish and Arabic legends it's six. There is also an old English proverb: "A cat has nine lives. For three he plays, for three he strays, and for the last three he stays." Many believe this is where the myth came from. But, to me, it just sounds like how everyone's life looks. When you are a kid you play; in your teenage and young adult years you travel, move around a lot and try to find yourself, go to college, backpack across Europe, pretend to like yoga, get tattoos you regret; and when you are older you settle and get a job and wait for

14

death. Do they have nine "lives," or do they just live on average to nine years old and some guy just planned his cat's life out like it was his son? You can play, then you become a doctor, and then you take care of us. That proverb is dumb. I'm just gonna say it.

I think it really comes from the fact that cats are pretty resilient animals. There's no better way to say it: they are expert fallers. My cat falls out of bed all the time. They have these reflexes that help them twist their body and safely land on their feet, plus flexible bones and ligaments which help avoid injury. Essentially, they have the body of a drunk driver. (You know how drunk drivers often survive car accidents because they don't tense up, as alcohol has made them loose . . . it's like that, but they are drunk all the time . . . I don't think I'm describing this right, but I am sorta alluding to your cat having a drinking problem.) But, in general, cats often seem to make it out of very frightening situations, cheating death more often than not. They are incredibly intelligent and intuitive. They have lightning-fast reflexes, quick decision-making skills, and remarkable dexterity. Cats are the extreme sports animals of the wild. Let's get them a Red Bull sponsorship!

Baby Killers, or Scapegoats for Bad Parenting?

A myth I've always known about is that you can't have a cat around a newborn cause they'll suck the air out of them. What? How can anyone believe this? Reports of cat-caused baby deaths are scarce, so how did this myth become so widely believed and passed on? One case in 1791 said, "A child of eighteen months old was found dead near Plymouth; and it appeared, on the coroner's inquest that the child died in consequence of a cat sucking its breath, thereby occasioning a strangulation." Logical conclusion. I think when people don't know the cause of death they blame who/whatever is closest. We now know that healthy babies can die without any known causes, often known as SIDS, but this just seems like when the room smells of farts and you blame the dog cause he can't defend himself. "The cat murdered my baby" defense is a bit suspicious.

Cats can be assholes, for sure, but them being givers of bad luck, ghosts that keep coming back, or baby killers is not any of the reasons. Stick to facts!

Now that we have that out of the way, let's dive deeper into why *your* cat sucks!

CATS ARE ASSHOLES, YES, BUT PRETTY LOW MAINTENANCE

Freshwater fish are the number one most popular pet in the world. (Weird . . . I literally know no one that owns a fish, but whatever). But number two is cats! (Then dogs, then birds, then giraffes . . . I dunno, I'm guessing.) I kinda get why fish are number one: they are pretty low maintenance. I had a fish named Archimedes when I was sixteen (traded a pair of my favorite wool socks for him . . . I truly think I overpaid). I cared deeply about him for like three weeks, then I kept forgetting to feed him. I became disturbingly relaxed about how often I cleaned his bowl. In my defense, he was crazy and kept trying to escape/kill himself every time I cleaned his bowl, and it was super stressful. I was also sixteen and barely a person. That being said, I did a shit job taking care of him for two years, but he was fine. Then I went off to college and I gave him to my mom and she fed him every day, changed his water every week. He died two weeks later. I was like, "Mom! He lived off neglect. He

16

thrived in neglect. He was used to neglect. He doesn't know how to survive in a healthy environment?" And that's why I excel at cat parenting. They don't *need* much. They're self-cleaning, box pooping, food regulating, mostly sleeping beasts. Pretty much Pet 101. I think a three-year-old could do a pretty decent job raising a cat.

And because they are so self-reliant and non-invasive, I think we let them get away with more bad behavior than we would a dog. Ninety percent of the time I don't see or smell them. It's like that annoying roommate you get used to because they pay the rent on time and spend most of the week at their boyfriend's place. Yes, I hate that my cat walks on the kitchen table when I'm eating and tries to eat my food, but it's a ten-minute battle and then we both go and get "work" done. (By work, I mean I watch YouTube while she watches a wall.)

> ## PET MATH
>
> **Loves me back + level of cuteness - how bad it smells / how much work I have to put in to keep it alive = if it is a good pet for me**

If I barely have to take care of you, you don't smell up my home and my stuff, and you're cute, your love barely factors in. I know you are thinking, *then why have a pet?* But my question to you is *why have a kid?* Legacy? Bitch, people shout out my cat's name at shows! Kids and larger animals (dogs, horses) are so much work it puts pressure on them to love you and show up for you, which causes resentment. Why do you think

kids go through a teenager phase? Hormones? They are just overwhelmed with living up to your expectations! Dogs chew shoes out of anxiety of being enough. My cat loses no sleep over our relationship—nor do I. Cats are both beginner- and advanced-level pets. Reason being, you don't need to know much to take care of them but you need to be mentally healthy to accept them as they are and not try to change them. Does that make sense?

FREQUENTLY ASKED CAT QUESTION

Question: Are cats really on this planet doing recon for an alien race planning an invasion of our world?

Answer: If they are, then they're sleeping on the job. If they are, then they might be doing it the way we work when we say "we are working from home" but are really in our pjs watching Netflix and occasionally answering emails. If you told me they were an alien race I wouldn't be shocked, but if you told me they were collecting data or trying to take us over I'd say we are safe. I think it's how most people feel about America in general. People that don't live here look down on us for being privileged, dumb, and fat—and they aren't wrong. But then they get here and they are like, "Dude, Amazon delivers anything you want, you can get burgers for a dollar at 11

(continued)

18

p.m., and every place has Wi-Fi? I get it now! I wanna be dumb and fat, too!" Cat aliens probably rightfully hated Earthlings and then spent a week with us and were like, "Uh, why are we trying to take over again?" Don't stress. Befriend the enemy. They give great snuggles . . . even if they occasionally remember they are on the job and bite us.

2

CAT JOBS
AND BREEDS

FROM FARM CATS TO SHIP CATS TO BODEGA CATS

Few things give me more pride than the long history of working cats. Everyone talks about how bomb-sniffing dogs save lives . . . but if their smell is so superior, then why don't they seem more upset when their farts could melt paint? Many of them go under strict and grueling training, and not all dogs are suited for this line of work. Some breeds are never even considered while others fail out of training. And let's not forget how many TV shows and dog schools are out there with the sole intention of training your dog to behave.

Cats have been used as cheap and efficient rodent control since the beginning of time (slight exaggeration, but you get it), and with *zero* training. And yes, #ALLCATS.

Cats are usually free *and* don't require training. Why aren't more people talking about this?! They are natural killers. Seriously, they are the Navy SEALs of killing tiny pests.

We already talked about their domestication and forever friendship with humans, but cats aren't just cute couch potatoes.

Oh, *My* Cat? He's in the Navy!

I refer to ship cats as the bodega cats of the sea. Ship cats were common on trading, exploration, and naval ships dating back to ancient times. Vermin could damage ropes, woodwork, and today electrical wiring, as well as eat crew food supply. Plus they were (and are) a source of disease. And rats on ships were believed to be the main spreader of the black death, so their natural ability to attack and kill rodents and their ability to adapt to new surroundings made them great crew members! Besides, that doesn't even take into account the fact that having a pet on board was good for morale and helped men have a sense of home and companionship. Sadly, since 1975, the Royal Navy has banned cats and other pet animals on ships due to hygiene, but they are still common on private ships. So out-of-work ship cats left the sea and started their new line of work of sleeping on bread in bodegas.

Bodega Cats

The blue-collar worker of the cat world. They are cheap and effective pest control for all the bodegas (delis/corner grocery stores) in NYC. So next time you see a cat sleeping on the produce scale or blocking a whole aisle stretched out, give them an ear scratch and a thank you pat! Yes, your chips are warm and crunched, but it's worth it to knowing they've been protected this whole time. My favorite Instagram account is @BodegaCatsofInstagram. I even have their shirt! It's just cats sleeping on food, inventory boxes, and ATM machines. Best content on the interweb. Go support their cuteness!

PUREBRED CATS DO EXIST

There are at least 102 cat breeds! Did you know that? I kinda did, but people don't care or fuss over cat breeds like they do dogs. They have them, but they don't matter (clearly my opinion). Most cats are just domestic short hairs or domestic long hairs (the cat version of "mutts"). There are purebreds, but I've never met anyone in the real world that has one. Who would pay for an animal not to pay attention to you? It's old rich ladies in movies and famous gay men (I'm looking at you, Freddie Mercury). Everyone else is finding their cat in a bush or something. I actually think that's why cats have a longer life span than dogs—they are mixed! They have strong genes and immune systems. Their ancestors ate the black plague. That's like if we all licked the subway poles every morning.

Honestly, even the breeds I do know I have my own names for them. Smoochy-faced cats (Persian), Naked cats (Sphinx), Envelope ears (Scottish Fold), Pretty Leopard-looking cats (Bengal), Fat cats (Maine Coon), Willy Wonkas or Dunkin' Donuts (munchkins), and Annoying cats (Siamese). If I knew more breeds I'm sure I'd have more made-up names, but I believe these are some of the most popular purebreds.

EVERYDAY CAT BREEDS

Because so many domesticated cats are just mutts, I've created my own breeds based on job descriptions, unique fur patterns, and cute disabilities. Feel free to use these breed names in your own life.

"Oh what kinda cat do you have?"

"A Pirate"

"Oh, is that a breed?"

23

"It is now!"
(high fives herself)

Kitlers

I didn't make up the term Kitler. I discovered a website about them fifteen years ago (think Tumblr heyday). and they've been my fav type of cat to spot ever since. They are usually white cats, or their face is white and they have a tiny rectangular-shaped tuft of black fur over their mouth that looks like a Hitler mustache. They make looking evil so damn cute! Some are truly spot on and make you worry that reincarnation is real. The background of my phone is a kitler I spotted on the streets in Bangkok.

Hipster Cats

A cat that wears their fur mustache ironically, or dresses in a way you would not expect. So cats with fur that looks like those old timey mustaches that curl up and it looks like they are a bartender in a western (or Brooklyn). Most famous is Hamilton the Hipster Cat. Or it could just be a cat that you dress up in an *Even Stevens* T-shirt. Hipster cats are both born and raised.

Sockheads

Like sneakerheads, but socks . . . you get it. I don't need to explain this further. Cats whose paws are a different color than their body. They are referred to as "having socks." Who doesn't love socks you can't take off? As sock culture has grown (it's my favorite thing to receive and give as gifts . . . fun ones, not ones you buy at CVS), it's nice to know your cat won't have smelly feet!

24

VET DAUGHTER NOTE

The cells that give cat fur its color slowly migrate down and around the body while a cat's embryo is developing. Felines come out having white feet, faces, chests, and bellies when these cells don't quite make it. Think of it as your cat printer ran out of ink.

Dressed to Impress, or Tuxedo Cats

I've always loved black and white cats, and there is something adorable about them forever dressed formally like they are going to an award show or an opera yet they are really heading to take a nap in a closet.

Pirate Cats

Cats that are missing an eye or a limb. I grew up with a one-eyed cat named Patches (named that cause it was a calico—don't be rude) and my sister's cat is missing its front leg due to getting hit by a car when it was a kitten. Pirate cats are the cutest cause when they bite you it feels like they are trying to steal your ship, too!

Make up your own cat breeds! If you have an idea or feel like your cat has been overlooked, send in pictures and made-up breed names by tagging me **@lizmiele** and using the hashtag **#WhyCatsAreAssholes**.

DRESSING YOUR CAT FOR SUCCESS

They say to dress for the job you want, not the job you have, and I'm not sure why that only applies to humans. If you want your cat to be taken seriously in the home, at the vet, or on the Internet, they need to start dressing better. Even if you aren't a cat poster (a person who posts cat pictures online), we all know cats love to sit in windows and wilderness watch. Why not let your neighbors know this isn't just a job to them, but rather a lifestyle!

Cat style is real and it will reflect on you, the owner. In 2019, WikiLeaks founder Julian Assange was arrested and charged with conspiring to hack into a Pentagon computer network. *However*, trending on Twitter that week was questions about what was gonna happen to his cat. His cat, Michi (but better known as Embassy Cat on Twitter and Instagram), was known for his eclectic tie wardrobe and people were very concerned about his wellbeing after his owner was arrested. I think the takeaway here is if you are doing shady shit, dress your cat up to deflect attention (and also get some "awesome points"). I actually think that's why so many villains in movies have a cat. Can someone be all evil if they take care of a pet? I think the logic is evil people = evil animal, but we all know that's not true. I believe the better logic is that even evil has some warmth. It creates complex characters. We all think of serial killers and psychopaths as having no ability to connect or show or receive love, and a pet like a cat shows that they are indeed human. It gives the audience something contradictory. They are also just good for morale. After a long day of things not working out, we all want something to snuggle with. All that being said, Cinderella's stepmom's cat was named Lucifer and was a huge dick, so sometimes evil people have evil pets. (Isn't it nice, at least, that they found each other?)

But I digress. A cat's outfit is something to think about and you don't need to wait for Halloween to showcase the fact that your cat has style. Whether it be a fun collar, a tie, a bandana around their neck, fun hats, or full ensembles, your cat cares about their reputation and so should you!*

---

*   My cat doesn't like or dislike being dressed up. She has an ador-able indifference. If your cat doesn't like it, don't do it. It takes an asshole to raise an asshole. Respect boundaries. And you'll know if your cat says "No" to clothes.

MY FAVORITE FAMOUS CATS

It used to be that the only famous cats were the ones we saw in movies and television, but now with the Internet, Instagram, Twitter, TikTok, and all the memes and GIFs passed along on them, any cat can be famous—and for the cutest and weirdest reasons. A few of my favs are:

Grumpy Cat (@realgrumpycat): famous for her perpetual frown and memes about enjoying nothing (RIP, she died in 2019).

Smudge (@smudge_lord): white cat from the popular cat meme mash-up of the *Real Housewives* woman yelling and the white cat in front of vegetables looking mad back.

OwlKitty (@owl_kitty): black long-haired cat really named Lizzy (just one Liz respecting another) whose owners remake movie scenes with her in them.

I don't know how you use social media, but I only follow my friends and cats. It's the perfect way to not let it ruin my day and actually feel uplifted. These cats inspire me to work harder and be more judgmental, and I thank them for it each and every day.

FREQUENTLY ASKED CAT QUESTION

Question: How can I help my cat with their self-esteem?

Answer: I get this question all the time. Your cat just doesn't believe in himself. He's not going for the jumps he could easily make. He's only taking up a quarter of the bed as if you didn't buy this huge mattress just for him. He captures a cockroach but can feel the cockroach doubting him and lets it escape. These are all signs of low self-esteem and need to be mended. I always say: A healthy cat is a cat that thinks it's better than you. Think big-dick energy, but for cats it's just cat energy. So how do you help your cat center themselves back into the kitty gods they are? Here are three quick tips:

1. Words of encouragement. People aren't the only ones that feed off compliments and praise. Leave your cat a note. Tell him "great chase today!" Scratch his butt when he does well. Let no good effort go unnoticed.

2. Cats need to feel loved, safe, and respected. Show love the way your cat likes receiving it. Kitty treats, tummy rubs, lap snuggles, high fives. I don't know your

(continued)

29

cat, but give a little extra if they are feeling low.

3. Set up some easy-to-accomplish goals. Finishing dinner. Burying poop. Crying at the wall. Things they already do, but let them know they are killing it. Sometimes you need a participation trophy to get you to the next level of goal setting. Be your cat's coach and biggest cheerleader!

3

THERE'S A MURDERER IN YOUR HOUSE

Both my parents are veterinarians and tell me stories about clients all the time. My dad told me recently about a new client that came in. He was just making small talk and he asked what she did for a living, and she said, "criminal forensics." He was like, "that's cool." Then she got really serious. "I just wanna let you know, Dr. Miele, dogs are loyal."

He was like, "What do you mean by that?" And she was like, "Well, a lot of times we don't find these dead bodies until three, four days later, and whenever there is a dog he just sits near the body and waits. Cats? Eating their face. Every time." and my dad is searching my eyes, like "that doesn't shock you?" And I was like "Shock me? Do you know how many mornings I wake up screaming I'M NOT DEAD YET!?" They don't love you! Cats are just tiny adorable terrorists that don't love you. If you want an open casket, get a dog!*

WILL MY CAT EAT ME WHEN I DIE? PROBABLY.

You know how when you are stuck underground on the subway for like ten minutes and you start to freak out cause you don't have any snacks, and you think, "What if we never move? What if we are stuck here for days? Weeks? Months? How will I sur-

vive? Who on this train will I eat?" Cats are like that too, but it's every day and starts at around 4 a.m.

Sadly, the rumor of cats eating their owners after they die has some validity. Cats truly won't wait more than a day or two without being fed before they resort to eating you. Hell, they won't wait more than five minutes from after they ate half their bowl to pester you for more. It's called "postmortem predation." But it's pretty in line with who they are. I can't imagine my cat waiting more than an hour after I die before she eats me. That's why I'm not donating my body to science—I'm donating it to my cat. I've come to terms with it. I don't judge her. She has my last name and a Facebook fan page. She is my legacy. She will carry our name two to five more years. I'm pretty sure, legally, she gets all the royalty money from this book.

I guess what I'm saying is, yeah, it's not a good look . . . but is it really that bad? To me, it feels like the ultimate form of recycling. I guess I get if you want a traditional burial where people see your body that might be a problem. However, I wanna be cremated, and so Pasta will just be saving my family time and money!

CATS ARE THE HUNTERS WE IMMORTALIZE IN MOVIES

Cats are hunters. Your miniature yorkie wouldn't make it a day in the wild. My cat would be the leader of a wolf pack in a weekend. They are tough. They don't have the reputation of nine lives because they are clumsy, they have "nine lives" because they are resilient animals and they take risks. They make bold, often unresearched choices, and with great risk comes a lot of physical close calls. I love all the videos of cats attempting

ridiculous leaps and missing. They are only funny cause the cats don't get hurt. But that boldness, that sheer "ah fuck it" attitude. It defines #cattitude. Animals with cattitude should be cats, people that do parkour, everyone in the X Games, and maybe turtles. They don't give a fuck and live forever! Also, side note: I think cats invented parkour. I've taken four classes and I think I can safely say my cat could teach me all the same moves.

All that said, cats even attack other cats and animals with a fearlessness that makes zero sense. Yes, I get annoyed and mad when my cat attacks my foot but, dude, I'm seven times bigger than her yet she still goes for the kill. That's pretty brave. I feel like that should be a meme. "Attack the day the way your cat attacks your foot—with zero logic and all heart!"

CATS DOMESTICATED THEMSELVES

They say that humans domesticated dogs over the span of many years, but cats actually domesticated themselves. Cats used to loiter and hang out at farms cause they attract prey and vermin, so farmers liked having the cats around because they killed those pests. It became a beautiful friendship that lasted the test of time. If you have a farm and you don't have a cat, are you really a farm? Yes, it looks like barn cats mostly lie in hay and on the backs of horses, but they are resting up to kill mice. That's the beauty of cats. They don't work hard—they work smart! Truthfully, they actually only consider pet cats "semi-domesticated" (which would make a great cat punk band name).

Domesticated Cat DNA Barely Differs from Wild Cat DNA

It always looks like my cat is hunting. She is. They are. They crouch down and attack your feet. They hide on top of the kitch-

en cabinets and fur-bomb attack you. Mine is a little black panther hiding, waiting for the least convenient time to ruin my hair or outfit.

While we all like to pretend our cats are just baby tigers and lions, they actually aren't. They are related to small wild cats, but not the big ones we think about. The African wild cat is the common ancestor to all domestic cats. Actually, the African wildcat DNA is almost indistinguishable from the DNA of domesticated cats—and they look similar. It's just that our

kitties have had years and years of living with humans and have gotten . . . well . . . lazier, friendlier, sillier. All that said, domestic cats are very similar to large cats. They have found that pet cats share 95.6 percent of their DNA with the Amur tiger. So, you don't necessarily have a wild animal in your home, but it's safe to say that many of the traits we love about our cats are found in the wild. I think that's why I love every picture online of a tiger in a large, cardboard box. It makes you think, *I could be a tiger mom. I'd just have to buy bigger things off Amazon.* Every tabby is a baby tiger. Every black cat is miniature black panther. Every black and white cat is a tiny cow. I'm lost. What was I doing?

MOM! I BROUGHT YOU THIS GIFT. IT'S DEAD!

My cat has presented me with three mice in our cohabitation together. Two dead, one alive that she was torturing in front of me. That number is low for a few reasons. Pheromones from cats alone actually send out a warning to mice to stay away, so I think households with cats have fewer mice, statistically. But if I'm being really honest, my cat lives a life of privilege and complacency and I've seen her play more with her prey than actually kill it. I'm not pro my cat murdering mice. But I am anti my cat torturing mice cause she doesn't know what she wants to be when she grows up. Kill it or befriend it (so I can submit it to those "odd friendship" sites), but don't *Saw* it for three hours. Not in my house.

I was once sitting at my desk writing and my cat was behind me crying, trying to get my attention. I was ignoring her cause I was busy, and she kept walking across my keyboard and I was over her keyboard butt prancing. So, finally, after her eighth or so cry, I'm like "What?! What do you want, Pasta?" I turn around and see her proudly standing over a little mouse toy . . . which I was kinda impressed by, as I had bought her these little mouse toys months ago and she lost all eight of them instantly under my bed, dresser, and couch. So I was like, "Cool, good for you! Happy you found a toy" and went back to work. But she kept crying, and I turn back around and noticed that the toy was moving. She had brought me a live baby mouse.

Shit.

So I go over and check to see if it's severely injured, and it looked fine. I gave Pasta a few minutes to decide if she wanted to kill it. (It was, after all, her "find," and I wanted to respect her hunt.) But she wasn't doing shit, and I didn't want this mouse in my house (sorry Dr. Seuss), nor did I want my cat torturing it. So I put it in a shoebox and I brought it outside. No idea if that was the right thing to do. I essentially told this mouse, "You're camping now! You're now on the mouse version of *Naked and Afraid.* Hope you survive."

My sister, Emily, told me she was once sitting, watching TV with her husband, and all of a sudden her cat, Avocado (the healthiest of the cat names!), sounded like it was choking. She runs over and there is like a string hanging out of her mouth, and she was indeed choking. So she pulls it out, thinking it was a cat toy and IT WAS A BABY MOUSE! STILL ALIVE! The mouse runs off and hides. My sister and her husband scream and hold each other for hours (I assume . . . I was screaming when she told me this part of the story) and Avocado just stares under the couch all night, giving random death glares to my sister for losing her after-dinner snack. Apparently Avo didn't move all night until it came out and she captured it again, injuring it, and then my sister released it outside. But what? Why didn't my sister teach her how to chew? Why is her cat swallowing a mouse whole? Why does she think she is a snake? How many other mice did this mouse tell that story to? Can this be the plot of a new *An American Tail* movie? Think about it. Mouse gets stuck in cat throat. Then, unharmed, runs off and tells friends (no one believes him, but he does smell like cat food so people start to come around) and the mouse . . . let's call him Charlie (mice seem like they have jobs, so they should have human names), knows the cat is waiting for revenge. Then tries to sneak out to start a new life now that he has street cred and his peers think he's a badass. He is now the mythical mouse that lived inside a cat (he would clearly embellish the story for effect—and to get laid). Then during his escape, he gets cocky and injured by the cat. While dragging his broken legs, trying to get to safety, he gets captured by a beautiful human then teleported to the wild.

I need funding. I need to make this movie! (Yes, Avocado is the villain in this story. She only has three legs. She's always had an adorable Captain Hook vibe.)

Bring Out Your Dead

They say cats—especially females—bring back dead or half dead animals to their kids to help teach them how to kill for themselves and feed themselves. I feel like my cat being named Pasta is like an Italian mother. She's like, "You're too skinny. *Mangiare, Mangiare!*" And then I was like, "I'm not hungry, Mom!" and threw my food away. No wonder my cat will ignore me for days sometimes. She brings me food she hunted and I'm like, "No, I don't want it" and she's like, "Spoiled brat. I cook, I clean. I sleep on your stuff, and this is how you repay me?"

We had a cat that lived at my parents' practice when I was little, named Patches. She was deaf and had one eye, yet was the most talented hunter I've ever seen. She'd bring back dead adult bunnies and birds as big as herself. Like, you'd show up to the cat clinic and there would be a dead bunny on the steps leading in. It was both creepy, unprofessional, and almost a weird ritual. As if Patches was blessing the practice. Also, my little brother, Greg, got a hunting license last year (we are not a hunting family at all) and a gun, and every Thanksgiving and Christmas will go in the mountains to hunt turkey. He'll go, "Ma, don't buy a turkey. I'm gonna bring one home!" and we all laugh cause hours later he'd be back empty handed, saying how he didn't even see one. He was too young to remember Patches, but I think she could have taught him a trick or two.

They also say spayed female cats bring gifts to their owners just cause . . . just cause? Maybe its customary the same way it's an unwritten rule to bring a gift when you go to someone's place for dinner. Maybe cats are taught that you should bring your owners a gift. Regardless of the reason, it's never a good way to say thank you when someone brings you a gift to:

- Be appalled.
- Throw it away in front of them.

Now I regret all the times I've disregarded my cat's dead mice as trash and not gifts.

If I did that to a gift my boyfriend gave me, he'd be like "I had a receipt. We could have returned it. Also, why'd you throw it across the room and start crying?" What I'm saying is maybe think about how your cat feels when they bring you a dead animal. They scoped it out for minutes (maybe hours . . . I mean, they have the time), they wrestled and killed it for you (or like, kinda traumatized it and it's kinda playing dead), and then they presented it to you. (They would have wrapped it but they couldn't find the wrapping paper. And the tape always gets stuck in their fur and while their nails do cut paper well it seems to be a challenge to just use one nail as an X-Acto knife like they do in kid's cartoons.)

I'm just saying, it's fucking thoughtful and you should treat it as such. Maybe try eating it. (Nope, just Googled that. That's definitely how people get diseases and die . . . but you could pretend!) Maybe hang it on the fridge. (Also a terrible idea . . . OK maybe draw it and then hang that on the fridge.) Maybe kill something for them (perhaps a neighbor you don't like).

You say you love your cat, but how are you showing it back!? It's like that love languages book. We show love by petting and holding. Cats show love by leaving us dead stuff and lying on our clean clothes.

KILLING IN THE NAME OF

Australia is currently killing off their stray cat population, as they are supposedly killing indigenous birds. Which isn't great, but I don't agree that the solution is to kill cats. How about find them homes, or teach the birds to fly higher or be less dumb? I don't know what the solution is but I find it so ridiculous that you'd kill a cat to save a bird.

I'm also anti kill shelters and I hope cat cafés and sanctuaries completely replace them. I understand there are limited resources, but it breaks my heart that animals are put to sleep because they simply don't have a current home.

FREQUENTLY ASKED CAT QUESTION

Question: Are all cats reincarnated murderers?

Answer: Honestly, it would explain a lot. There are some bat shit crazy cats that might just be no good. Like if they look like Scar from *The Lion King*, I wouldn't trust them with my life. But I think the truth is you live with a hunter. Cats very much still resemble their wild ancestors and while sometimes they attack a fly or a stuffed animal and it's adorable to you, it's a very real threat or food option for them. And when they attack you it's because they have big egos and thought they could take you. Maybe do some pushups in front of them or knock their toys off the shelf. Show them you are tough. Try alpha humaning it and see if they see you as an equal.

4

KITTENS—FUR BABIES OF TERROR

I'm actually the daughter of two veterinarians . . . which I thought was awesome
when I was a kid, but now I know they are they are just psychopaths that only kill
pets. I fully believe all veterinarians are just stunted serial killers, they just never
graduated to people. They didn't apply themselves. Cause you have to understand
that I have an old sister who's a nurse, so she has probably accidently killed people.
That's human error. That shit happens all the time. My mother, on the other hand,
is a cat specialist. My mother has purposely killed hundreds of cats. Fluffy starts
peeing on the carpet? You don't want it anymore? That's on you. Don't put that
on my mom, she's an angel! I'll say this, though: She's been doing it for over thirty
years. She's jaded. She's starting to say some stuff I don't agree with. I called her
up a couple months ago and was just complaining about my cat. I was like, "Ugh,
she threw up on my bed. I just did my sheets. I'm so mad right now!" She's like,
"You want me to kill it?" I was like, "Mom!" She's like, "What? I have a kitten in
my office right now. You could start over with like a cuter, better, more resilient
cat." I was like, ". . . well, is it available?" She's like, "No, but I'll just tell them it
has whisker cancer. They don't know."

I love kittens. Truly nothing makes me happier, but I feel the
same way about kittens that I do about babies. I like holding
them for an hour and giving them back to whoever made the

mistake of owning one. Kittens are just furrier babies with razor blades taped to their paws. They are like tiny wolverines.

You have a kitten? Well, get ready to lose sleep and blood. I often look at pictures of my cat as a kitten and think, *aww, she was the cutest.* But if I'm being honest, she was the worst for a full three years, and like a new mom in the middle of the night, I'd question my life choices. "Why didn't I just get another tattoo? It could have been of a cat. I'm Italian. Very hairy. No one would know the difference."

Cats sleep sixteen to twenty hours a day, but for some reason almost none of those hours are when you sleep. The best thing you can do for your sanity is get them on your sleep schedule. My cat as a kitten would be asleep during the day and attack my face at night. To fix that I did what my parents did with my little brothers growing up: sleep deprivation. (Is it technically torture? Yes. But so is the sleep deprivation they are inflicting on me, and I have a job so it's a little bit of torture for the greater good.) We'd be on a long drive and my brothers would fall asleep in their car seat and my dad would say, "Don't let them sleep. I don't care if they are crying, but don't let them sleep!" Because they were trying to get them on their sleep schedule. So I took that to heart and did the same with Pasta. I'd come home from class and she'd be asleep on the top of the couch and I'd wake her up and bother her. She'd be grumpy, but I'd still play with her and annoy her a bit. Every time I saw her sleep during the day, I'd wake her up.

Two things happened:

1. She started to hide when she took a nap.
2. After a few days she started to see me crawl into bed and would jump in with me and curl up for the night. It

was both the cutest habit and the most rewarding. It's still our pattern fourteen years later, and my bed is filled with cat hair to prove it.

TINY WOLVERINES

Another awful thing about kittens is they have knives attached to their paws and use them for everything. I don't wanna say they don't know how to use them, because they do. But like an older cat knows there is a time and a place and a kitten is like a child

that got a new toy and wants to use it for everything. There's no sensei to sit them down and be like, "Hey, nails are for killing bugs, mice, climbing trees, and opening mail. That's it. They are not for climbing up legs, sending a message about dinner not being on time, a way to wake up a sleeping friend, or how you get on the couch." It feels like you've given a toddler a samurai sword . . . and they do the damage you expect they would.

Clearly, trimming them is key (you press their toe so the nail pops out and you trim *only* the white part. Pink is skin and you will hurt them/they will bleed and you will lose their trust). I personally don't think it's hard to cut cat nails, but some kitties are wigglers so don't be shy about getting outside help. Scratching pads are also a great way for them to naturally wear down their nails and save your furniture, and if they are ruining your furniture and your life you can put on nail caps. There are clear ones, but also some with different colors. Think of it as nail polish for kitties. They cover the nail, rounding it so they are less harmful. Clearly this is for indoor cats. Outdoor cats need their claws to climb and fight bears. Don't de-weaponize them.

RAISING THE CAT YOU WANT

All this being said, you're raising your future friend. Yes, cats all have their own personalities and quirks, but if your cat hates you my first question is "what did *you* do?" Cats can be dicks, but many grow up to be loveable lumps . . . and if yours is trying to hurt you, my first thought is "hurt people hurt people," and it applies to animals. Animals that lash out usually have a reason. The same way humans deflect pain by reacting with rude, mean behavior, abused cats will retaliate as well.

If you have a kitten, think of them the same way you would raising a child. Am I making a good person (cat)? Am I making a person (cat) that makes a positive impression wherever they go? Does your child (cat) make you proud? If someone met

your child (cat) on the street, would you be embarrassed by their behavior?

You think I'm being silly, but I genuinely feel good when my cat gets a good report card from friends that watch her, people that come over, or when she stays at my mom's clinic. It's a reflection of you and your relationship with your cat. I get "your cat is so friendly," "she's so sweet," "she loves to cuddle while I work," and I'm like, *yeah I did that*! Took years, but she's the kitty daughter I can be proud of! Shower your kitty with love and attention now so that they can shower it back at you later.

But kittens are also gross, and some can be untamable demons. I'll admit that. Lemme tell you a story . . .

Back in college, if you would have asked me if I was a cat person I would have said, "My love for cats is unconditional. They are just the sweetest, coolest, cutest animals in the whole wide world." (I would be squeezing Pasta at this moment, and she would be biting my face to express she would like to be put down . . . I would not see the irony.) I had Pasta about two years at this point and she was still a bit rough around the edges, but we had learned to live with and love each other as we were. But this story isn't about Pasta. This is about a kitten named Kyle. (I think that was his name. If not, that's the name I'm giving him to protect his identity, as it's a douchey name. Sorry all my friends named Kyle.)

My roommate, Michelle, at the time:

- never liked cats all that much
- is mildly allergic to cats
- suffered many a battle scar from fights with Pasta

Why Cats are Assholes

She started to come around and like cats—mostly cause I would squirt her in the face with a water gun every time she complained about Pasta. Now when I came home they were cuddling on the couch (usually her rolling a sticky lint brush over Pasta's body to catch the hair before it falls, playing together, or attacking each other but with love).

Michelle started to become a cat person, whether she wanted to admit it or not. She has always been a big dog lover and used to foster dogs once or twice a month, but the shelter she was working at moved away and she was looking for another place to foster animals. She ended up starting to foster kittens once in a while from Petco.

I love kittens. It was always hard because I would fall in love with every kitty, beg my roomie to keep it, and then two days later it would be gone. I never had a problem with her fostering cats. Our place smelled a little worse, our stuff a little more broken, our nights a bit more restless. But they were cute—it was overlooked.

My roommate always gave me a heads up when she was fostering.

"Hey, I'm bringing two kitties home. Is that cool?"

"Hell yeah! Yay kitties" was always my response. So it shouldn't have been a surprise that one morning when I was getting up and making breakfast, instead of one kitty sitting on the counter waiting to try to eat my eggs, there were three. I wasn't mad. It was no big deal, but I was a little thrown off. On my counter sat Pasta, and two tiny orange and white kittens. One of the kittens she fostered the previous weekend and apparently didn't get adopted, so he was back. I wasn't surprised, since he was the devil. He's the type of cat that ends up in a box on the side of the highway. You think, "oh that's awful how could you say such a thing? . . . well, you don't know Kyle. I used to think that was unthinkable, too. He is a wolf in sheep's clothing, and I, for one am not fooled.

I scooped eggs from the pan onto my plate and started putting salt and pepper on them. All three cats inched closer, putting their noses close to my plate like I didn't know what they were doing. Kyle, caring only about himself, was just about to leap onto my plate until I pushed him away. That's when I noticed that something smelled bad. Like, real bad. I couldn't figure out where it was coming from. I grabbed my plate of eggs and began looking around to try and see if one of the kitties had an accident somewhere in the kitchen . . . but I found nothing.

I wanted to eat my breakfast, but the smell was revolting and my appetite was fading. I was just about to move to my desk in the other room when I saw it. On Kyle's back left leg, smeared and caked on, was shit. Not only was I not hungry for food anymore, but now I was going to be late to work because I had to clean Kyle's ass and leg before I left (plus all the places he'd walked around the apartment). I didn't want him rubbing his shittiness all over my stuff.

So I grabbed Kyle and tried to hold both his back and front legs with one hand and took him to the bathroom sink. I don't need to tell you how Kyle felt about this. Before I even turned on the water he was struggling to get free, and as soon as a drop of water touched him he went nuts. Just flipped the fuck out. All I wanted to do was rinse the poo off his leg, it's not like I wasn't trying to waterboard him. But he acted like I was trying to drown him and then skin him. He was writhing back

49

and forth, scratching the shit out of my hands and arms. He was splashing water everywhere and trying to make his way out of the sink, but with each attempt I'd push him back under the faucet getting a little more poo off, but now adding blood to the poopy mix. Kyle flipped out so bad that he knocked just about everything around our bathroom sink into the gross sink water—including our toothbrushes and Q-tips. Finally, I gave up. He was clean enough. I released him and he flew out of the sink and ran away.

I quickly wrote a blood- and shit-splattered note to my roommate, who was at the gym before work. "Kyle shit all over himself, tried to wash it off—was not successful. You also need a new toothbrush." I looked around. There was mucky brown and red water all over me, the sink, and the floor. Blood was dripping down my wrists and nasty toothbrushes and Q-tips were everywhere. I was angry, hurt, and late for work.

I changed clothes, put Band-Aids on all my scratches (which were throbbing), and ran to work.

For a bit of background, I had been working as a temp on and off for almost two years at a convention-staffing place when stand-up was slow. I was touring a little and had not needed to temp in over a month, so this was my first day back. When I entered the Javits Center I saw all my old work buddies and they all came over to say hi. I was exhausted and still mad from the morning and was a little out of it and couldn't return their enthusiasm. They looked down at my wrists, which both had huge band-aids on them.

Christina looked concerned. "Oh, um . . . so, how have you been?"

"There's good days and bad days."

50

Kyle broke me. I will never look at kittens the same way again.

FREQUENTLY ASKED CAT QUESTION

Question: How much of my value as a person should I base on the way a cat reacts to my presence?

Answer: Seventy to ninety percent of one's value should be based on how any given cat receives you. I fluctuate daily. It's a real rollercoaster of emotions, but we all know you are only as good as how the last cat feels about you. That's why it's helpful to maintain a happy and healthy relationship with your cat. If you have low self-worth, maybe it's time to talk to your cat and see what you can do to strengthen your relationship.

5

DOES MY CAT HATE ME, OR IS IT JUST TRYING TO RUIN MY LIFE FOR FUN?

Cats have this rap of being super clean and, for all intents and purposes, they are. Bathing is a daily ritual for them and they legit get in those toe crevices with a spirit that is bordering on OCD. It's impressive and I salute them. I think they are the least smelly pet because of their due diligence. I can tell when I walk into someone's home if they own a dog or a ferret on smell alone. I don't think that's true for cats. But they do have some gross behaviors that, while annoying, I've dealt with a little too well.

WHO'S GROSSER?

I'm a gross person. I don't wanna be gross. I wish I didn't eat in my bed. I wish sweeping was a weekly (uh, monthly) activity. I wish I didn't have to hype-man myself to get into the shower most days. I do, however, always put it on my to-do list to feel a basic level of accomplishment every day. #LifeHack

53

I don't know if this is some mild form of depression or just who I am intrinsically, but I think this OKness with being gross is what allows one to be a good pet owner—especially with cats.

Yes, cats are the "cleaner" of the pets, and my cat is no exception. I've had her for fifteen years and I think I've bathed her like five times during some travel mishaps (that's the nicest way I could say, "vomit and diarrhea all over herself" . . . I don't want to shame her in publication and then get sued by her fans, so let's just continue to call it "travel mishaps"). But, for the most part, she spends a good portion of her day self-cleaning. I honestly think her to-do list is:

- Sleep: 16 hours
- Bathe: 1–2 hours
- Wind sprints: 1–2 hours (but only between the hours of 1–4 a.m.)
- Stare at a wall, out the window, or at Liz: 1 hour (crying while doing it is optional)
- Destroy everything Liz loves: 3 hours

My cat cleans herself well, but often while making my living space grosser. My cat is so smart I refuse to believe she doesn't know what she is doing. Let me count the ways she has ruined everything I love.

WHERE SHOULD I VOMIT? WHEREVER FEELS COMFORTABLE, MY LOVE!

I take great pride in (mostly) vomiting in the toilet or a nearby bin I placed next to my bed when I was scared I wasn't gonna

make it to the toilet . . . at least in my adulthood; I've been told I was less accurate as a child. Exception being when I got my wisdom teeth out when I was twenty-one and the medicine made me nauseous and I projectily (I don't know if that is a word but I stand by it) vomited across the bathroom, hitting only the wall above the toilet. (Two of my siblings watched in awe and concern . . . it's talked about to this day . . . true exorcise style!) All I'm saying is if you love yourself or the people around you, you try to make wherever you vomit as easy to dispose of as possible. Not cats. Cats vomit where they are at that exact moment. Not considering that it's probably their favorite place to nap or MY FAVORITE PLACE TO NAP, PASTA! They vomit on bathmats, in closets, on couches, carpets, on their beds—which is often *your* bed. If they sleep there, they probably also vomit there.

My cat sleeps either next to my legs or next to my head at night. And when I'm not home, she sleeps smack dab in the middle of the bed. This is important to note because when she vomits it's wherever she is sleeping. So, she sits up straight and starts making the retching sound every cat makes. It's like the bat signal, but to warn owners of gross danger. I'm a light sleeper, thank god, and when I hear it I instinctively pick her up while she is dry heaving and put her on the ground (I have hardwood floors) so that she can vomit on something easier to clean up . . . and then I go back to sleep.

I know, I know. I told you I'm gross. But I'm tired and don't wanna get up and get paper towels and Clorox wipes and clean the floor, then tie up the trash then wash my hands. So she vomits, I go back to sleep and forget, and 70 percent of the time I step in it and hate her and myself. BUT it's better than the bed. I will take ruined socks over a ruined comforter every time!

Why Cats are Assholes

This is how gross I am, and I'm so ashamed to admit this. She's vomited on the bed and I've folded the blanket over it and gone back to sleep. I'M TIRED, BACK OFF!

Yes, I'm a disgusting human, but if she needs twelve to sixteen hours of sleep, I need to get my seven to eight, and this shit can be weekly! Also, hairball vomit isn't as gross as food vomit. It's pretty odorless (mostly mucus and hair) and you often can't see it until you slip in it. Whatever, I'm a single cat mom doing the best I can! And because it dries clear and I travel a lot, sometimes she vomits on the floor and days later I'm like *what the hell is that*, and it's a hardened hairball rock (think *Jurassic Park* mosquito trapped in sap, but its hair trapped in stomach mucus and is less majestic and holds the key to nothing). So when that happens, I boil water and pour some over the hardened hair and that helps lift it and then I make it into a tea . . . kidding, kidding. That's gross, but it does make it easier to clean up. Just a little cat lady life hack. You're welcome. Other solution might be some kind of cat hairball Roomba. That needs to be invented. I don't have the time or resources, but if they can self-vacuum can't we figure out how to self-mop? Inventor people get on it!*

> ### VET DAUGHTER NOTE
> While hairballs are normal, food vomit isn't normal and can be a sign that your cat isn't OK. Please alert and see a veterinarian if your cat continues to vomit. Also, please call or see a vet.

---

* Apparently it *is* a thing . . . who wants to buy this for me?

I PEED ON YOUR FAVORITE DRESS. IT'S A STATEMENT PEE.

My cat has also peed on everything I love. It took years of heartbreak to learn not to leave anything I care about on the floor (much like how some dog owners hide their shoes) because a bag or a pile of clothes is soft enough to lie on and, if they lie there they might pee there. I remember the first time Pasta peed IN my backpack. You heard me. Crawled in my bag, pissed on all my schoolbooks, and then left me to find it. I've been dumped and cheated on and felt less betrayed. It's mean to pee on something, it's *fucked up* to pee *in* something. I mean, how do you look anyone in the eye after they pee *in* your stuff? She peed in my bag. I was like nineteen or twenty and I washed it thoroughly. As I'm sure you know . . . it did nothing. Still smelled like pee cause cat pee isn't just pee, it's like pheromones mixed with asbestos and nail polish remover. It's potent. It needs to be cleaned carefully, and there might be some causalities. It's like trying to get gum out of your hair. You can do it, but it might not be the end result you were looking for. It was a free backpack from a corporation and my first pee experience, so I just threw it out. But as the pee tally went up and the items got pricier (mattresses, nice dresses, shoes, people), I learned how to properly clean cat urine. So now when my cat pees on stuff, I clean the item and the area with Nature's Miracle just for cats. (There are other brands, but that's just the one I like. No one's paying me to say that. It just works well for me.) What these fancy sprays do better than detergent alone is eliminate stains and odors and discourages cats from peeing in that area again. So I wash the floor with the spray, let it dry, and then later wash with regular floor stuff, then I wash the item again in just the spray. Then I rewash with detergent and then I grow up and stop leaving my clothes on the floor. Last part is the hardest. I've bought so many hooks as a compromise.

Also, let's just say it. When your cat pees on your favorite dress, you start to question the phrase "unconditional love." You start to think there should be *some* conditions. If my boyfriend peed on my favorite dress cause he was mad at me, I'd probably let him know this isn't the best way to communicate. Be normal . . . cry and scratch my face like an adult! God!

But as I've learned from some of our pee issues, sometimes she's acting out but other times peeing on stuff or outside her litter box can mean health problems—urinary tract inflammation, diabetes, and kidney disease being some common reasons. So never just assume your kitty hates you. Most likely it hasn't been to therapy and doesn't know how to properly express their pain. We've all been there, Sprinkles! I got you!

STOP TOUCHING MY STUFF!

If a baby might be fascinated by it, so will a cat. My cat has played with and grabbed necklaces and dangly earrings. Gone nuts on a sweatshirt pull string. Has attacked shoelaces like they stole her wallet. It's both adorable and dangerous. I've always wanted a vanity where I'd keep my make-up and hair products out for easy access and cause I'm lazy, but I can't because everything is too "rolly" and fascinating and brushes are apparently too similar to mice if they were attached to sticks. (My cat's words, not mine.) And I guess hair ties look like stretchy bugs that need to be taught a lesson. I have lost sooo many make-up brushes. Maybe they remind her of her mother when she'd put on make-up in the evenings before going out on the town. I dunno. But she's stolen so many over the years that I now keep all my make-up in a large zippered pouch and even when I stay in a hotel, I put all my make-up back in the pouch when I'm done out of habit and fear. Most missing make-up brushes have never been found again, which is a mystery I will never solve. My cat steals them. I've caught her sooo many times in the act, but sometimes I'm in a rush and leave them out and, sure enough, I come home and they are gone. I search all her napping and hiding spots—under my dresser, in between couch cushions, in the closet, under the bed. Half the time I never find them.

When I was like nine or ten, my younger sister, Emily, had a hermit crab and we were playing with it in the basement on the floor and looked away for what felt like ten seconds (but we were kids and it was probably more like three to twenty minutes). Whatever, it was so fast that it ran off somehow and we never found it. Searched everywhere. It was one of these weird childhood mysteries in our family. Then we moved a few years later and found it in this side room/closet where we kept random office supplies and toys we rarely played with. If you mapped out our basement from a hermit crab's perspective, it would have been the equivalent distance of the US to Japan. The fact that it walked there was crazy! We never checked that area cause it was unimaginable. He was found under some toys . . . clearly dead and dried out. But it was kinda like one of those tragic wilderness stories. Guy unsatisfied with his job and boring normal life searches for meaning roughing it on his own in the woods. Our hermit crab searched for a way out, unsatisfied with his life in a tiny clear box with one stick and an ugly shell with Atlantic City painted on it and being randomly tor-

59

tured by dumb kids. He thought he could make it on his own. He looked for food, but all he found was fax paper and old McDonald's toys and eventually died alone under some blocks.

I always remember finding him. We completely underestimated how far he got and though sad, having an ending to that story was satisfying. It taught me that sometimes you have to wait and see how things end. It taught me patience and how morbid my family was (as we laughed about it).

So when I moved from my last apartment five years ago, I was kinda excited to finally find out where my cat actually hid all these make-up brushes and whatever other loot I wasn't focused enough to know she took. But I never found them! Did she eat them? Does she have a secret vent she dropped them into? Is she like a dealer in a prison? Does an alley cat pick these items up every few weeks? No idea. It's still a mystery to this day. I like to think she's writing her own book about it. *How to Get Away with the Purrfect Crime*, *Brushed by Fate*, *Mad About Make-Up*. I dunno. The real shocker is when I find out she's been making make-up tutorials on YouTube this whole time. "So that's how she gets that perfect cat eye every time!"

YOUR STUFF IS IN MY WAY. DON'T WORRY, I KNOW WHERE TO PUT IT.

I've woken up so many nights to my cat pushing something I love off my desk or dresser that it would be a welcomed relief for it to be an actual burglar for once. I'd be like:

a. I have no valuables, my cat has stolen or broken all of them, and
b. Please take the cat with you. She's also great at stealing stuff!!! She truly could be a partner in crime!

The Internet is a treasure trove of cats pushing things off ledges because they are curious about how gravity works or they just like to fuck with you. There really are two types of cats.

Scientific cats—I call them "Newtons"—who push stuff off ledges but seem to be genuinely interested in what happens. It feels like they are taking notes. Like, "OK that one shattered. Interesting." They pay attention to every detail of the procedure . . . how the item moves when they push it, how long it takes to fall, the sound and what happens on the floor. It's frustrating, but it feels like a kid doing a project for their science fair. Yes, they set the drapes on fire, but how else are they gonna learn?

Why Cats are Assholes

The second are evil cats—I call them "Captain Hooks," cause of the nails and their cold hearts—who push things off tables with malicious intent. They look deep into your eyes and push objects over the edge to see how you will play your next move. They know what happens when it falls, they have zero reaction to the crash sound and they know they shouldn't be doing it. My cat has been on this earth for fifteen years. She's a grown-ass woman who knows that things crash and break, yet she's gonna pretend she didn't know? NO! No. Some cats are just clumsy. Tails too bushy and unruly to control, but I'm talking about the paw push. The *tap tap tap* to the edge move. I think 80 percent of cats do it as a power play. "Oh, you wanna wake up at 9 and feed me like I haven't been up since 4 a.m.? Well, Liz, then maybe this potted plant no longer having a pot will make you think about your choices."

I'm also a clutter bug. I love knick-knacks and junk and trinkets. My desk is covered in every sticky note I've ever bought, pens, encouraging notes, pictures of friends (and my cat, obviously), and robot and animal figurines. My dresser is the same plus hair products and jewelry, and most days I find half of it on the floor because either my cat felt it was in her way or just wanted to know how it could turn into twenty tiny pieces. My favorite move is when she's jumping from the bed to the dresser and there isn't a cleared-off-enough landing strip for her when she makes the jump yet seems unbothered and unfazed by the fact. She's just gauging if she can make the jump itself, not the area of where she's landing or even factoring in the momentum of her jump . . . so she lands and then knocks over half my stuff, and I feel like a mom cleaning up after her kids have come home from school and dropped their stuff everywhere in the hallway. Like, "Guys, every day?! Do you have to do this every day?! We talked about this! This is a home not a youth hostel! Am I talking to myself?"

WHY DO THEY WALK OVER ME LIKE I DON'T EXIST? IT MAKES ME FEEL LIKE A GHOST.

I'll be completely asleep and my cat will walk over my ALIVE body like I'm a stuffed pillow under the covers only there to trick my parents into thinking I didn't leave the house. It's weird. She knows it's me. I even think she knows I'm sleeping but walks over my body and my face while sleeping, or my hands while I'm working on my computer. It's a level of rude that when she does it, I impulsively do that passive aggressive thing you do to people when you are so angry you can't not react. I'll out loud say to her, "Ohhh, I'm sorry. Was I in your way?" But I'm not sorry. I'm mad. I was asleep. And now I'm awake. And you stepped on my mouth! I'll never get over that.

You know how they say dogs can sense when you are sad or sick, and they come over and comfort people? I think cats possess the opposite ability. They sense your immune system is compromised and they have the advantage. The amount of times I've had a stomachache and my cat has jumped on my stomach because she didn't see me as a living breathing thing is insane. I think my cat sees me in pain and thinks, *This will be mine soon. Let's see how much meat is on her!* She'll stare into my eyes like a witch doctor trying to determine how long I have left to live. Its impressive, really.

By the way, no one really knows why they do this. I looked everywhere and every veterinarian, every animal behaviorist, is like, "they don't see you as important" or "you are so much bigger than them they think you can take it." It's like the baby brother effect where they punch you and then they are like, "I'm just a tiny boy. How could that hurt you?" And you're like "Cause it's my eye, Sam! It's my very sensitive irreplaceable fucking eye!"

So that's my conclusion. Cats are baby brothers that never grow up and move out. Sorry. I'm sure there is some way to try and teach them not to do this. I personally think I sleep on my stomach now because it hurts less. Honestly, this is one of those weird moments where I'm like, *I might have to change.*

When I was little—I think around six—I shared a room with my older sister, Theresa. (I'm one of five kids, by the way. By now you are probably like, *how many siblings does this cat lady have?* I'm the second oldest of five. My mom literally made a litter of humans.) My dad bought us these tents you could put over our twin beds, and I was obsessed. I loved it. It felt like I had my own room and space. I did everything in there, and I bring this up because maybe us cat owners might need to buy them now. Just saying. Seems like a fun solution, and then you can like tell people you are going camping and take selfies and then pretend your cat crying is a bear. I think I really solved this!

THE PROS AND CONS OF PEEING INDOORS

I LOVE that I don't have to walk my pet three to five times a day in the snow at 2 a.m. Whenever I am having a mental fight with my cat, I remember that she's pretty self-sufficient. It's like having a twelve-year-old. She's potty trained, rations the food I leave out, can entertain herself, and I don't feel too guilty leaving her alone for hours (read: days). But I think the biggest struggle people have with cats is the litter box. I know it is a struggle for everyone because there are four new litter box inventions every year for the last five years. Automatic litter boxes, litter boxes hidden in everyday furniture, litter boxes with fancy tops and doors, litter boxes in fun colors that look like a giant kid cube with a hole at the top, the sifting layered litter boxes to make cleaning easier. Then there are all the litter mats to catch the litter debris and the different types of litter so your room doesn't smell. For as clean and self-sufficient as cats are, their litter box is a never-ending puzzle. Few things are as upsetting as stepping on random kernels of litter barefoot, and few things are as embarrassing as the strong smell of a cat's fresh poop when you have company over.

One of the most embarrassing memories I have was when I was twenty-two. I just started seeing this guy (we dated for three years, so we got over this hump I'm about to share). I don't know if we had even kissed yet or we just kissed that evening but were flirting and sitting on my couch in the living room watching a movie . . . minutes into it my cat gets up and takes a huge smelly dump in her litter box, which was across the room right near the TV. Filled the room with epic poop smell. So I got up and, as sexy as possible, had to go scoop litter in front of this dude and bag it up. Why, Pasta? Why then? It's mean! I'm trying to find you a cat dad. Jesus!*

Also, I feel like there is no good spot to put a litter box. If you keep it in a small room, it's destined to always smell. If you put it in a bigger room you will always be sweeping up

* He went on to love her and carry her while he did errands around the apartment and I converted him into a cat lover. He got his own cat a year or two later. So, temporarily, they had a lovely father-daughter relationship. They no longer speak from what I am aware of.

and scooping. I've bought enough things that it's pretty much under control, but my cat goes through these burying/kicking litter out of the box phases that is just messed up. She's even "accidently" kicked her poop out. I know people that keep it in the bathroom cause it is technically a portable toilet but stepping on litter barefoot is just too awful for me. I actually bought two litter boxes and put one in my room and one in the hallway so that I could regulate which one she used when I had guests over. They also now have those bins that you can throw clumps and poop in right away and throw out later that trap the smell. I think they make them for diapers, too. That has been helpful. I'm so pro buying every cat litter invention there is to make that problem less of a pain. (Except the automated one. Most cats are too skittish and are anti robots so I think that one was good intentions with no cat focus group.)

Thankfully, my cat does bury her poop. Nothing is worse than a cat that doesn't bury it. That's like having a roommate that doesn't flush. "Come on, John! I don't wanna be this close to you?"

Your cat is your roommate and they gotta start showing some house-sharing etiquette! My cat didn't bury when she was a kitten and I took her little paws and showed her how to do it. That's what mom's do. They get dirty. They show them real-world skills. If your cat doesn't bury, maybe you need to get in there and show them.

MIELE FAMILY STORY EVERYONE BUT MY BROTHERS ARE ASHAMED OF

I think I was already in college, so my brothers were around eight and nine years of age. We had an unfin-

ished basement. There was a couch and some chairs, a TV, I think a foosball table in the main room, and then doors with a kitty door that led to storage and the boiler room, and that's where the litter box was. My parents kept two litter boxes side by side so that if they forgot to scoop, our cat, Max, had options. Is it lazy, or did my cat live in a house with two bathrooms? Luxury. Anyway, my mom kept bringing Max into her practice because he was peeing excessively. So much so that there was urine at the bottom of the litterbox and she was worried he had some extreme kidney issues. But every time she checked, nothing was wrong. She was puzzled. Then she discovered my brothers, too lazy to go upstairs, were peeing in the litter boxes (and when we moved also found out they were peeing in the toy closet). BOYS ARE GROSS! So there's no point to this story other than to shame my now adult brothers.

SHEDDING: WHY CATS AND WOMEN GET ALONG

I'm a shedder. I find my hair EVERYWHERE. I'm constantly surprised I'm not balding cause I just don't understand how I still have hair. But I feel the same way about my cat. If she lays down *anywhere*, she leaves behind a pile of fur. But she's also a creature of habit, so she has a few spots she always sleeps in and if I don't wash them or lint brush them there is this dryer lint drawer amount of fur that is both impressive and gross. I found several Esty shops that sell cat fur dolls and I'm shocked everyone doesn't recycle their pet's hair that way. Also, it could be the best "fuck you" gift to a frenemy that's allergic to cats.

Why Cats are Assholes

"Oh Sarah, I got you this doll." <Weeks later> "I've been having trouble breathing. I'm not sure why."

I remember when I first got Pasta, my dad bought me this Tempur-Pedic pillow that I just didn't like. It was weird and, like, too stiff for me, so I gave it to my cat. It sat on the chair I had in my room next to my bed, and that's where Pasta slept most of the day. Then my sister, Theresa, and brother-in-law, Rob, came to visit me for my birthday, and I gave them my bed to sleep in. Rob, who has a minor allergy to cats, wakes up the next morning and is like, "I don't know. Cats have never bothered me this much, but my eyes and face itch sooo much. I guess it's gotten worse." Turns out he grabbed Pasta's pillow on the chair, not thinking anything of it, and slept on it. In the morning I showed him his mistake. It was truly a pillowcase of fur. I was in college. I think I hadn't washed that pillowcase in two years. I'm surprised I didn't kill him.

My favorite shedding story: I was on the L train going to an internship in college and was sitting down, but the train was packed and this tall man wearing a grey business suit stands in front of me. I look up and his crotch is directly in my face, but it's covered in cat hair. Just a big cat-size circle of hair, and I found it both embarrassing and adorable at the same time. I fought the urge to pet it, because they make announcements about how that stuff is not OK—even on the train—so I resisted. But I wanted to stalk him and be there for the first person that was like, "Glen, you need a lint brush or trimmers, brah! Cause you are hairy!"

CRY ME A RIVER

So, this was a really important year for me. It was around my fifth year of seeing a therapist, which is significant for me because I fought it. I fought it so hard. I wanted nothing to do with it, but now I'm glad I'm in therapy. It has really opened me up, because it has made me understand why I say and do certain things and why I've made some of the biggest decisions in my life.

Actually, the biggest decision I've made is doing stand-up. I started when I was a teenager and I always thought I did stand-up because I hated my family, but it turns out that I do it because I'm a product of mental illness and abuse. And I don't blame my parents because they are a product of mental illness and abuse. And I have a cat and she is a product of mental illness and abuse. She has to be, right? I'm the only person that could have fucked her up. I've had her for her entire life. I got her as a kitten, little five-week-old kitten. She fit in my hand and, within a few hours of having her, I realized I got the wrong kitten. She sucked. I thought I had an unconditional love for cats until I met my cat. But now it's like nine years later and she's great. She loves me. She sleeps on my face. She follows me from room to room. She actually has to be in the room that I'm in at all times because if I shut her out, she cries relentlessly on the other side because she thinks something awesome is happening on the inside. I have created a cat with some of the worst abandonment issues I have ever seen that I only recognize because they mirror my own. And I tell you all this because I probably did the most psychologically fucked up thing a couple of months ago and I now know I have nobody to blame but myself.

I screamed my cat's name out while having sex.

That happened.

And before you judge me, it wasn't passionate. It wasn't like, oh, Pasta. It was more like a divorcee mom that hasn't been fucked right in a while. It was angry. It was mean. I scared even myself.

And it escalated in a way that I don't think I'll ever be able to accurately describe. Because what happened is I brought this dude home and I shut the

69

door because I have roommates and I'm a good person. And within a couple of minutes, my cat starts crying outside the door and I don't know what to do because this is my time. I'm not moving, I'm not getting up. So I start with the first thing I could think of, I started with the Cesar Milan, the dog whisper. The shh, shh, shh. And I think this dude thinks I'm orgasming but failing out at the last moment. He has no idea what's happening. So eventually I just scream, "PASTA" right in this dude's ear. And . . . he did not call me back.

KITTY CRIES AND WHAT THEY MEAN

Not all cats are criers but, if they are, they seem to be relentless. The same way parents start to understand the different messages in their babies' cries, I've started to discern my cat's cries. My cat also became more vocal as she got older. I don't know if it's cause she learned that I respond to it, but it started to get really bad after she turned twelve. The tough thing about cats is they are smart. If they cry at 6 a.m. to be fed and you feed them, they now know that tactic works. So, they keep doing it. I once leaned over the bed, grabbed a shoe, and threw it at the wall to try to scare her quiet (I was desperate . . . and don't worry, it wasn't near her) and it worked for a minute . . . and then she went back to crying. They learn that your shouting or throwing stuff means you are awake. And if you are awake, then they are one step closer to being fed. It's tricky, but you can't ignore all cries. Cause some really are cries for help.

- **High pitched and quick:** I've probably accidently stepped on her (obviously). But, man, is that not always a shock to us both. I didn't see her. She didn't plan on being almost murdered. Sometimes I chase her around the room apologizing, trying to pick her up and smother her with love so she knows it wasn't on purpose. But other times when she sees I'm walking back and forth doing something with urgency and falls down in front of my feet so fast I don't have time to avoid stepping on her, I'm like, "Yeah, that's what you get! We talked about this! I'm busy. I know you see that!" And then I feel bad and apologize to her under my breath. Yeah, I know I shouldn't have kids. I'm aware. But human or cat, high pitched is shock/pain.

- **Long, drawn out cries:** Hunger. That, or she's practicing a song I hate. I hear it in the morning when I'm still sleeping and right when I get home after work. *Meowwwwwww. Meowwwwwww. Meowwwwww.* "Come on, dude. You aren't starving." She has a bowl of dry food always out and full, plus we have bugs she can eat. She's just being dramatic. Also, the routine is pee and then go feed her. I'm not torturing her, I'm never doing my taxes, then curling my hair, then re-organizing a closet, then feeding her. It's the second thing I do in the morning and when I get home. It would be the first, but I have a small bladder and she needs to accept that.

- **Quick, repeated cries:** She wants to be let in or let out of a room. It sounds like a carbon monoxide detector that ran out of battery. *MEow. MEow. Meow . . . . . . Meow.* My cat often gets up with me in the morning and will follow me into the bathroom, and she'll either sit and watch me pee or sit on the toilet and listen to/watch me shower, but if she was slow and didn't make it into the bathroom by the time I shut the door I'd usually start hearing her cry five minutes into my shower.

Sometimes I'd have to get out of the shower and let her in because I didn't want her to wake my roommates. My roommate Carmen once posted a picture of my cat sitting outside the bathroom door crying with the caption: "The line for the bathroom is so long."

FREQUENTLY ASKED CAT QUESTION

Question: Can cats see things we can't?

Answer: Ghosts

6

RESTING CAT FACE

If dogs always look happy to see you, cats seem to always look disappointed you are the one who entered the room. There was a nice three years where my cat greeted me at the door. That phase was short lived. It was around the time she was diagnosed with cancer, and I think the realization that she might die made her change her outlook on life and be a better cat—not just for me, but for herself. But then my mom cured her and now she's fine and has reverted back to her old, selfish tumor-less ways. Now when I enter a room her ear slightly twitches and I think she also sneaks a sly peek, sees it's me or smells it's me, and does not move from where she is sleeping. I'm happy she trusts that I am not a threat. That feels like a solid pet owner/pet parent accomplishment, but the lack of acknowledgment or excitement for coming home feels like a never-ending teenage phase I was unprepared for. I guess as long as she's not doing drugs and getting weird forehead tattoos I should just leave her be.

Cats are notorious for looking like you just gave them a parking ticket even though they were just dropping off their son at school and were only gone for three minutes. The truth is that dogs have more muscles in their face than cats, which is why cats are less expressive than humans and dogs—so it's not their fault. They express their feelings more in body language and sounds. And what's even harder is the same body language can mean something different in certain situations, so you need to be more in tune with your cat's feelings and surroundings to truly deduce what their actions mean.

IS MY CAT HIGH OR ABOUT TO ATTACK . . . ?

If your son or daughter comes home with super dilated eyes, they are on something. If your cat's eyes are dilated, it's either afraid or about to attack/hunt something. Which, if you are a teenager that does drugs, you should just attack a feather or puff ball and say you are in hunting mode. (Honestly, that's only gonna give away that you are super-high . . . I'm sorry, I don't know how to help you. But do take a pic with your cat so it looks like you guys are twins!)

The notorious *dilated eye* often referred to as "puppy dog eyes" (no fair!) means a few things:

- Eyes wide and large pupils usually means trust or just being attentive
- Unblinking stare can mean control, dominance, aggression
- Dilated eyes with ears flat usually means fear
- Dilated eyes with ears twisted back usually means aggression

Typical Cat Eye
Slit pupil can mean fear, anger, pleasure, or excitement, so you kind gotta read the situation. Droopy eyelids/eyes closed is friendly, loving. It's basically the smile of the cat world. That's

why blinking slowly at a cat is a great way to communicate you are not a threat, but instead friendly and open to interaction.

I KNOW YOU HEAR ME!

Ears and sound are so important to cats, it only makes it funnier that they don't respond to their name or directions. Their ears move back when you talk as if to say, "I hear you, but I don't care." They twist like an owl's head to hear your footsteps or shouting better and then determine that they could probably take you in a fight and don't get up or move. It's impressive. It's cocky. It's infuriating.

When their ears are pressed down, though, it's a sign that they feel threatened/annoyed and are gonna attack. My cat goes from "I love this" to "you will pay for this" in a split second, and what's saved me from losing my hand is paying attention to her ears. If they are regular and pointing up, she's at ease. If they start to flatten, I have two seconds to move my hand. I know my cat so well that I've pulled friends hands away just in time. And sometimes she stays in the #mood for a bit, so leave them be. We all need time to cool off after a bar fight. Be sure to give your cat space to count to ten and make a grateful list before interacting again.

A TAIL OF TWO EMOTIONS

Let's talk tails. They are a key to a believable cat Halloween costume, but so hard to remember to lift when you go to pee! Am I right, ladies? OK, but seriously . . . most of your cat's mood can be determined in the way they carry their tail.

A kind of a *loose tail up while walking or nudging* means a calm and happy cat, but if the tail is up and fur fluffed out with

back arched means it's scared or angry. Think rub up against your leg cat vs. Halloween scary cat. You see the difference.

Note about tails: My cat has this habit of sitting on my chest (butt closest to my face) and then swishing her tail and hitting me in the face, or I'll be sitting at the kitchen table working and she'll jump up and walk past me, hitting me in the face with her tail. And I've asked my mom, "Does she have control over her tail?" and she was like, "yeah." So they fucking know what they are doing. It's like when you're at a bar trying to get the bartender's attention and then some tall dude stands behind you and leans over you like you aren't there. And you are like, "Hello?! What the fuck do you think I was doing?" (This might just be a me/short person thing.) But still they know what they are doing. My cat knows she's annoying the shit out of me and distracting me. She pretends like, "Oh shit, sorry, my tail has a mind of its own." But it's not an empty backpack on your butt. You fucking feel your tail hitting me. I think this topic triggered something in me and I apologize. The point is . . . they fucking know. So you know . . . use that info how you'd like.

THEIR TAIL—DO THEY HAVE CONTROL, OR NOT?

YES! They have to! I refuse to believe they don't. The Internet has all those little info-graphs showing what it means when a cat's tail is curved, straight, hair sticking on end, in between legs, etc. So, if their tail is the Morse code of limbs, then when my cat walks by and hits me in the face with hers she's gotta be doing it on purpose. I feel like this logic is sound. Cat tails are weapons of annoyance used to distract and infuriate owners. Tails: butt decorations, or soft police batons?

GENERAL QUESTION FOR THE PUBLIC: IF YOU COULD HAVE A TAIL, WOULD YOU CHOOSE TO HAVE ONE?

My answer is yes, I would. My reasoning: They are great for balance and controlling your jumps, so as a former gymnast, four-time parkour class taker, and frequent tripper, I think it would be really helpful for me to have one. I also love the ability to slyly hit people with it. Just from wearing them at Halloween parties from ages six to thirty-four, I can tell you they are just fun to play with and pet. Downside is I feel like it'll be like being left-handed—you'll need special toilets and pants and no one will make them correctly for a long time. Even so, I still think it might be worth the struggle. Oh, and this is all contingent on if it looked like a cat tail (fluffy and pretty). If it's gonna be scaly and gross like a rat's tail, I'm out. I don't care how useful and cool it is, if it's ugly and I have to cover it in tattoos to like it then it's a no-go.

Would you get a tail? Lemme know. Tag **@lizmiele** and use **#WhyCatsAreAssholes** via IG and Twitter.

79

HOW DO YOU KNOW WHEN IT'S SAFE TO PET A CAT?

The short answer is, you don't. As someone that used to suffer from pretty bad mood swings, I kinda relate to the erratic nature of a cat's temperament. One second they are in your lap pounding your hand with their head to get you to pet them and a split second later they are attacking your hand (with violence most of us save for zombies) with what feels like no warning.

But there is. It's subtle. The way you know a friend is mad at you via text by how they stop using emojis in their response, or how a boyfriend or girlfriend is hiding something by how they are smiling slightly too much? The signs are there, you just have to be on high alert, though most people are petting cats passively while doing something else. If you are watching a movie, you can't see the slight pull back of their head, the ears flattening, their body stiffen. The invitation to pet a cat is obvious and most often disruptive and aggressive. The motion to stop petting is like a sneaky one frame they put in Disney movies that are sexually suggestive Easter eggs. If you aren't looking for it, you'll miss it. This is all to say that you are petting cats wrong. The same way you make mistakes when you multi-task, you leave your hand susceptible to holes and blood when you pet passively. Like life, you need to be in the moment. Hands ten and two (on cats that's head and lower back above where the tail meets), watching their eyes close, listening to them purr. That way you can witness when they open their eyes, the humming stops, and they open their mouth to truly bite the hand that feeds them. Cats are not afraid to piss off their provider for being affectionate one second too long. You gotta respect it.

HOW TO UTILIZE HISSING IN YOUR OWN LIFE (YES, I'VE HISSED AT PEOPLE)

The most tell-tale sign your cat feels threatened or is mad at you (or others) is by hissing. Think of it as the equivalent of saying "I'll kill you in your sleep." It sends the message of anger and rage pretty efficiently. When a cat hisses they arch their back, their tail puffs up, they try to look big and tough, they bare their teeth, and the sound of butter hitting a hot pan comes out of their mouth. It's actually quite scary, and cats are carnivores so their teeth are made of tiny knives. They hurt. Even if you never met a cat before, you know the first time you see and hear this they are pisssssssssed. It's why I've innately hissed at people when words have failed me. You should try it.

Boss: Can you come in on Saturday?

You: *hiss*

Boss: Oh, OK. Never mind.

[End Scene]

Why Cats are Assholes

I bet they'd never ask again. Yes, a rumor will spread that you are crazy, but is that really bad? I've hissed at my sister, my boyfriend, people on the subway, you name it. You get results in one sound/zero words. Bonus points if you bite! If fight club was an underground group of men hitting each other to feel alive, then I wanna start "Hiss Hobby." An above-ground group of people hissing at each other to send the message, "I'm not friendly. Don't sit next to me."

FREQUENTLY ASKED CAT QUESTION

Question: Can cats really see in the dark?

Answer: No animal can see in total darkness, as you need some presence of light for the eye to see. They can just see better in semi darkness than humans can. They aren't seeing fine detail or rich color, but they have a high number of rods in their retina that are sensitive to dim light and so can see more at night than us. Hence when it's bright out their eyes are those creepy slivers and in low light and at night are wide and angelic.

7

TREE DWELLER VS. BUSH DWELLER

Thanks to Jackson Galaxy, we now have language and understanding of a unique attribute to domestic cat behaviors that we didn't always understand. Is your cat a tree dweller or a bush dweller? Well, it's important to learn this by observing your cat so you can accommodate what type of personality they may have.

I think of it the way we like to identity ourselves as either introverts or extroverts. I've always broken it down that introverts need alone time to recharge and extroverts need to be around people and socialize to recharge. Much like cats, they have behaviors they partake in to recharge or escape. Tree dwellers like to climb and be above everything to feel safe, while bush dwellers like to hide and be low to feel safe. Kitties don't come with manuals, so it's up to you to take in their behavior and help them feel comfortable and safe.

My cat is kinda a mix, but I'd say she's 80 percent tree dweller. She loves to climb up to the top of cabinets and the fridge and sleep up there. Every apartment I've moved into, the first thing she does is find the highest place she can get to and scope it out. If I can't find her, she's up top somewhere

sleeping. But when she is scared or noise is overwhelming to her, she likes to sleep in my closet (I started leaving blankets in there for her because she used to just sleep on top of all my shoes . . . how is that comfortable, Pasta?), or just wants to be close to me and will compromise and crawl under the covers of my bed and sleep there.

How you accommodate their needs is really up to you. I'll be honest: I've never bought a cat condo or cat tree. I've lived in tiny NYC apartments for over fifteen years and so never really had the space for them, but the one benefit of tiny apartments is everything is kinda cramped together so it was never really hard for my cat to jump from the counter to the fridge to the cabinets, and I made a point to leave clear landing and sleeping spaces in all those areas so that she could. And as for bush dwellers, you could buy little cat beds with roofs or cat tunnels, but if you don't want your floor to look like a tiny cat town you can just make the furniture you do have more inviting or accessible, e.g., I keep my closets open/ajar at all times, and you can keep the space under your bed and couch clear.

FREQUENTLY ASKED CAT QUESTION

Question: Do cats get embarrassed?

Answer: I've never seen a cat embarrassed. They get angry, scared, worried, curious, confused, sleepy, indifferent, and murdery, but I don't think they get embarrassed. To be embarrassed means they would change and do things differently, but my cat has been licking her butt too close to the edge of the bed and fallen off hundreds of times. She's never learned. Nor has she ever been bashful afterward. Confused, maybe. Like, *Who pushed me?* But never ashamed. She gets back up and goes to the same spot on the bed. There are theories, though, that when a cat immediately starts cleaning after doing something embarrassing that that is indeed how they feel/a cover up.

8

HOW TO NAME YOUR CAT

You might think naming a cat is hard, but you'd be wrong. It's actually super easy, yet people mess it up all the time. Bad news: if you give them a bad name, they will live fifteen to twenty years with it, which is a long time to explain your terrible logic and backstory of how they got that name. Good news: they will never respond to it. So if you are smart, you will hold off the cat name memorabilia until you are sure you both wanna live with the name Princess Meowjasty a fifth of your life and all of theirs.

Before we go into best practices and tricks into picking the perfect cat name, let's start with some naming no-nos.

NO MORE SIMBAS AND TIGGERS

If I meet another cat named Simba so help me God I will call the police on you for animal cruelty! Enough! *The Lion King* came out twenty-five years ago (I refuse to watch the live-action one). Move on! I never wanna meet another man named Steve or another tabby cat named Tigger. We are better than this! BE BETTER! How do you expect your cat's Instagram to go viral when they have a basic bitch name? Take your pumpkin spice latte of a cat name and start over. (Note: Pumpkin and/or Pumpkin Spice Latte are great cat names.) No one's going to college, so get creative and have fun!

> ## CAT NAME STRENGTH TEST
> **Simba:** ——Weak
> **Pumpkin:** ————— Moderate
> **Pumpkin Spice Latte:** —————Strong

IF YOU CAN'T SHOUT IT IN FRONT OF KIDS OR OUT THE BACK DOOR, MAYBE IT'S NOT A GOOD CAT NAME

My friend growing up named her cat Pussy. She was a child, and *Puss in Boots* was a book her mom used to read to her, but her parents were adults that told her no to candy for breakfast and should have said no to this, too. But they didn't.

Fast forward to us being fourteen. It's about to rain, and her mom is screaming "Pussy" out the back door and I can't sink any lower into her couch. Just no. Not cause it's crude or wrong, but because it's funny for like ten seconds and then you have to make vet appointments and it's just uncomfortable for everyone involved. Think of others but, really, think of your cat.

My parents have a client whose cat's name was "Shithead," so every year they have to call up the owner and say, "Hi, Shithead is due for their vaccinations." Don't get me wrong, it's hilarious. But it's also heartless. This is a beautiful beast, and it deserves a name people aren't embarrassed of.

88

So no to Pussy, Shithead, Poopy Face Fart Bottoms. I think you can go too far with the naming of pets. The Internet exists now. Maybe focus-group your name ideas on Instagram or ask some friends on Facebook before you name your cat Poo-Pourri!

Now for how to properly name your cat (and really any animal):

BE ADORABLE AND DELICIOUS . . . THE KEY TO GOOD PET NAMES

What's your favorite food? That's pretty much a great cat name! Go nuts, make it plural. Tacos, French Fries, Pizza, Pop-Tart, Oatmeal, Burger King, Honey Buns, Muffin, Waffle, Pancakes. If you'd be judged for naming your child it, then it's a perfect cat name. (Oddly, Apple is a terrible cat and human name—and I stand by that.)

My cat is named Pasta and my sister's cat is Avocado, or Avo for short. I've never gotten anything but compliments, and added bonus, their name and image is on everything. I saw at the Meow Parlor, a cat café in NYC, that they named a cat "Unlimited Breadsticks," and I've never been prouder of my community. Be crafty, dig deep. This is like a tattoo that will last fifteen to twenty years. It represents you. It represents your family. It represents your cat. If it's gonna ruin your furniture, it should at least be fun to yell at. "Goddammit, Quesadilla. We talked about this! Not the love seat!"

Cats With Degrees Are the Cutest!

Maybe food isn't your thing. Try going formal. Give your cat a degree or title. Mr. Bubbles. Dr. Fur Bottoms. Their Majesty Marbles. You don't know what they do all day. Who are you to assume they don't have a degree in psychology or medicine?

Why Cats are Assholes

Characters, Celebrities, and Backstories

There is a scene in the first *Toy Story* where Buzz Lightyear is missing an arm, is dressed in a women's sun hat, and is attending a tea party with dolls because he's trapped in Hannah's room (Sid's sister). She named him Mrs. Nesbit. When Woody tries to save him and he's having a mental breakdown and Woody is yelling "Buzz! Buzz!" he yells back. "It's MRS. NESBIT!"

Me and my sister quote that all the time. She'll be saying my name trying to get my attention. "Liz! Liz!" and I'll turn around, "IT'S MRS. NESBIT!" Never gets old . . . and that's why my next cat boy or girl will be named "Mrs. Nesbit." It's just fun. I love the idea of correcting people. Friends come over. "Here Nesbit. Come here, Nesbit," and I sternly correct them. "It's MRS. NESBIT. They have a husband. He lives elsewhere." (Yes I'm being a bit hypocritical since I said stop naming your cat Simba then said I'm naming my next cat after an equally old animated character, but this name isn't overdone. I've never met a cat named Mrs. Nesbit, yet I've met 500 Simbas.)

I never met my grandfather on my mom's side, as he died when my mom was ten. But his name was Casmiro, and she said he went by Casey. (Big mistake, if you ask me. The cooler nickname is clearly "Caz.") All that said, I don't know if I'll ever have kids, but I do hope to someday meet a cool enough cat to carry the name of "Casmiro." If children can have namesakes, why not pets? If I do have a kid I will probably name them after Pasta, cause her legacy also deserves to live on and I just have to pray my kid turns out nearly as awesome as her!

And don't forget that sometimes it's fun to just name a cat after a known person, as it's an ode to them and their work and just funny and confusing to others.

"Bill Murray shit on the carpet again."

"I had to put Jada Pinkett Smith down yesterday."

And who says they have to be a celebrity. Maybe name your cat after your friend. Make hanging out confusing.

"Michelle, get off Michelle. She's allergic."

I guess what I'm really saying is why not name your cat after me? I'd be honored, and promise to shower her with gifts!

Name for the Fur Pattern They Have, Not the Fur Pattern You Want

Sometimes the best inspiration you can have is what your furry friend looks like. How is your cat permanently "dressed?" Do they look like they are wearing socks? Does he/she look like they have a mustache? A hat? A tuxedo? Any fun or weird fur patterns?

Ideas:

Looks like it's wearing a tuxedo = Bond, Kitty Bond

Looks like it has a big mustache = Ron Swanson

Looks like it has a beard = President James Garfield

Has a '70s vibe somehow = Fur Reynolds

Looks like it's wearing socks = Risky (Full name: Risky Business)

Calico fur pattern = Rorschach

Has little spots = Moles

Stripped/tabby pattern = Zebs (Short for Zebra)

All black = The Witcher (Full name: The Witcher, Season 1)

CAT NAMING EXERCISE

Write your best names of the following cats, then take a pic and post on Twitter or Instagram tagging **@lizmiele**, plus use the **#WhyCatsAreAssholes** hashtag—most creative names will win prizes!

1. All black cat with a white fur line over eyes that looks like a unibrow
Answer: _____

2. White cat but two front legs are black from paw to mid shoulder (looks like it's wearing knee high boots)
Answer: _____

3. Orange long-haired cat with a white fur patch on its belly that looks like a heart
Answer: _____

4. Calico kitten with orange, black, and brown spots over a white body. Brown on head looks like bangs or a bowl cut.
Answer: _____

5. Orange tabby with white fur on chest that looks like he's wearing a tie
Answer: _____

FREQUENTLY ASKED CAT QUESTION

Question: What do I do if my cat doesn't like her name?

Answer: Well . . . how old is your cat? Does the cat respond to their name ever? Was this cat given this name by another family? Do you see them scribble different names in cursive in their notebooks? A name change, whether they respond to it or not, is serious. Letterhead has been made, collars have been bought, friends have been notified, but some names are just bad and can have psychological effects on your cat if they are made to answer to a name that just doesn't represent them. So if they aren't too old and they seem to be pretty indifferent when you shout it then yeah, change it.

9

CATS IN BOXES AND OTHER WEIRD TRAITS

IF IT FITS, IT SITS

Everyone knows by now that it doesn't matter how expensive the toy or how comfy the cat bed, nothing really replaces a cardboard box. My form of recycling is leaving out the box my new shoes came in in the middle of the floor and letting my cat sleep in it until it falls apart. It's like the slow version of cutting it up. When I was in college I bought eight tall glasses for my new apartment and the box had a peep hole to show what the glasses looked like, and my cat lived in that box for four years. She was a kitten when I got it and literally grew out of it. She would also bite all around the peep hole, I think as a way of tailoring it to her growing body. At the four-year mark her butt started to get stuck when she would crawl in and she had less and less room to turn around inside to the point that it became comical—until she eventually sprawled out and broke it like the storage closet scene in *Ace Ventura: Pet Detective*.

95

If Your Cat Doesn't Love Boxes, It's Broken

I think the pictures I love the most of Pasta are her in boxes—Amazon Prime to my suitcase. If it's a box with some stuff in it or empty, my cat's personal mission is to try it out. Like a mattress to a human, they just have to jump in and test it out. Unlike Goldilocks, it feels like no box is too big or too small. They all seem to make every box "fit." But the question remains: Why are they so drawn to boxes?

It's a predatory behavior that helps them conceal themselves and stalk their prey (prey being your feet, another cat, a sock they found, etc.). From what I understand, boxes help give cats a clear vantage point. They are physically protected from all four sides, they are able to get low and hide and keep an eye on danger, and it's just sooo cozy. Who doesn't like a cardboard hug?

Boxes are kitty fox holes. Cats feel protected when they are in boxes. I also think that whatever we are paying attention to, they are drawn to. If you are packing, they get in your suitcase, if you are opening a package, the get in the box the package came in. Every time I open a large envelope, my cat will put her face in it like a nosy neighbor—"what's that?"—then after I remove the item she crawls in, slowly turns herself around, and then pops her head out like a little manila envelope sleeping bag. I feel like I have more trash laying around my apartment because my cat adopted it as a bed for ten minutes and I didn't want to ruin her day. She comes back from a nap in my room to the living room like, "What the fuck, Liz? I don't throw out your tiny apartments whenever you leave the room!"

TRENDING QUERIES

Why Are Cats Terrified of Cucumbers?

I'm sure you've seen the videos. It looks like someone just left a cucumber on the floor, cat walks in or turns around, sees it, and freaks out like a *Looney Tunes* character. I'll admit, their reactions are so insane I was curious to find out more. Are all cats this skittish around boring vegetables? Is it a safety issue? Are they allergic to cucumbers and can't even be near them? (The peanut allergy of the cat world?) Do all cats react like this? Is it mean to do this?

As you can see, I had a lot of questions. I guess I don't eat a lot of cucumbers around my cat, as this just wasn't something

I'd ever encountered. Apparently cucumbers have a snake look and vibe, and this is their very real reaction to a predator in their home. Essentially, you are giving your cat a mini heart attack, like when you scare your spouse in the shower or put a fake roach on your mom's desk. I find it crazy that their reaction to a predator is so uncomposed and chaotic since they are the chillest of animals in all other situations, but all that said I don't think it's nice to spook your cat for amusement. Cats can be dicks, but don't be a dick back.

Do I Have Ghosts, or Is My Cat Just Meditating?

While it makes me laugh that I'll come into my room and my cat has her back to me and is staring at the wall for what feels like hours, it also freaks me out. I'm like, "dude, if we have ghosts you gotta tell me." Other times it feels like my cat is meditating, and I get jealous. I'm like, my cat sleeps and meditates all day . . . is this why she seems so content with life? What apps is she using? Is it the one with the British voice? Personally, I just don't find brits soothing.

But they aren't ghost hunting or meditating. If your cat is staring at a wall, it could be for a few different reasons. For instance, they could see and be tracking something you don't see: a bug, reflecting light, silly string that's been up there for two years. Or they could be hearing stuff you don't hear. Literal neighbors—or wall neighbors. People often find mice or rodents in their walls because their cats spotted them first with their ears. Gross, but also kinda helpful, too. Next time you're caught daydreaming and staring at a wall, you can be like, "uhh, I'm wall monitoring and I think we have a pest problem." #hero

All Cats Are Morning People

My cat still to this day does wind sprints at around 3 a.m., or sometimes I just catch her staring and watching me sleep. Neither are encouraged. As someone that:

- doesn't do mornings, and
- judges early morning joggers (I'll jog, just not before 11 a.m.), it's hard to understand that I technically raised a morning person (kitty)

Cats are nocturnal and do some of their best destruction while you sleep. I would never wake up thinking I'm being broken into or burglarized because that's what it sounds like most nights because of my cat's evening exercises. If someone broke in and knocked something over, they would just hear me yell "Knock it off, Pasta!" and be able to continue to take my stuff. (I have zero things to take, by the way. I think no one's ever broken into my house cause I literally have nothing of value. The first time I sublet my apartment I was like, *Shit, I need to hide my valuables*, and then two seconds later I was like, *Oh, I don't own "valuables."*)

But I digress. Cats sleep during the day because they do their best work at night. As a comic, I kinda relate to this. But we still don't keep the same hours.

99

FREQUENTLY ASKED CAT QUESTION

Question: Are cats liquid?

Answer: Cats are the snakes of the mammal world. They have almost no bones.* They seem to mold to any container they squeeze into and are often more fluff than fat and can squeeze under or in between stuff, giving them the illusion of having Alex Mack–like superpowers. (Is that reference too old? Well, it's from the Nickelodeon show *The Secret World of Alex Mack*, and she could turn into a puddle because she was poisoned and now had superpowers ... great kids' show in the '90s.) Anyway ... yes, cats are probably a liquid. I'm in talks with all of science right now to re-identify them as such.

*   Obviously untrue. In fact, cats have more bones (244) than humans (206). Cats have special bones in their vertebrae that have flexible elastic cushioning on their disks that make them smooshier (that's a science term).

10

LIVING WITH CATS—THE LONG GAME

I seem to be the go-to person with friends, co-workers, and fans who, when they suddenly get a cat or are thinking about getting a cat, have all these questions. The biggest concern, either because of the rap cats have for being distant or because they brought a cat home and it's been hiding under the bed for two days, is, "Is this cat ever gonna like and/or love me? Am I gonna have an angry gremlin sneaking around my house forever?"

Yeah, but not forever. It takes time. Sometimes a week, sometimes a month . . . sometimes even years. I know that's not the answer you want, but think about a real friendship. Sometimes you just click with a new friend and you are on the same page from day one, and sometimes a strong friendship grows slowly over time to the point that you can't remember when or how you became close, but you just are. And, just like friends, there are both kinds of cats. I've met cats that as soon as you sit down they jump in your lap and claim you as their human, but many cats are the latter. They've been hurt. (They were gods once, remember?) They are skeptical of humans. You gotta earn their trust, love, and vulnerability. And if you put in the work, like, 70 percent of the time it works out.

PUTTING IN THE WORK

First off, it's not much work in the beginning. It's more a waiting game. If a cat is avoiding you, darts out of the room when you enter, hides under the couch, doesn't come out till you are sleeping, that's fine. Don't force them to be out if they aren't comfortable or ready. Just make sure wherever they are hiding the most has what they need close by: food, water, litter, toys, a cozy place to sleep. Make it a safe place and let them do their thing.

When they do come out and you are around, DO NOT CHASE OR APPROACH THEM. Like a teenager, they gotta come to you. Them coming out when you are around is the first sign of trust, but it's not full acceptance. You can ignore them or give an across-the-room head nod, but keep doing your thing and let them be. One of two things will happen. They will either eat, drink, pee, and leave, or they will eat, drink, pee, and maybe observe/linger. And this is the slow beginning of them starting to trust you.

"But I wanna pet and hold them! That's why I got them!" That's why we all got them, Sarah! Fucking patience! Who raised you? You will, just maybe not today. Over the week or weeks they will start to see that your home is a safe place where no one is trying to hurt them and that all their needs are met, and thereby start to let down their guard and then opportunities to pet and hold them will come about. Even then, you gotta learn your specific cat's boundaries. Many cats hate their belly rubbed. Some love it. My cat hates her paws touched. This will

104

be a trial and error of pulling away, swatting, hissing, kicking, scratching, and so forth to show what they like and dislike.

Listen, if you don't abide by these rules then you start to break their trust and it will take longer for TV time cuddles. My cat was kinda an aloof asshole for three years. She hung out, slept near me, let me pet her, but never wanted to cuddle or sit in my lap. It made me sad cause I wanted a cuddly cat. So over time I just slowly inched closer and closer. Never being too aggressive. (Kinda not true . . . my roommate once came home in college to me hug-abusing my cat, yelling, "why won't you love me!" Even sadder, I've had that same exact fight with boyfriends.) But for the most part I respected her boundaries while slowly pushing them, too. All cats have a different temperament and acceptable level of affection, but you can also train them to an extent as well.

How to Kinda, But Not Really, Train a Cat

They do what they want . . . that's why they are so funny. They sleep in weird positions, in odd places, on unconventional objects. They walk over you and your family as if you are furniture. They cry incessantly when they want something. They are said to be untrainable. But that's simply not true, just Google "Moscow Cat Theater" (It's like a cat circus. It's my favorite thing. You are welcome!)

You can train your cat, it just takes real work and most people don't want to put in the work. At some point you decide, "how much does this really bother me?"

For some reason, dogs are taught tricks with a reward system. You do this task you get a treat, but because cats are so skittish, more people try to teach cats with the punishment

system. This doesn't really work, and if you do it wrong you are really just teaching cats not to trust you or to be fearful in your home, and that's not kind or helpful if you want to have a calm, cuddly, healthy cat.

My dad taught me that if I wanted to keep my cat from jumping on the table or kitchen counter to get a small spray bottle and spray her with water every time she jumped on the table. But the key was you had to do it without her seeing it was you. If they know it's you then they won't care. They need to think some ghost is haunting them with water so they'll become freaked out by counters. But it's really difficult to not be seen. Her eyes are so big, she always heard me coming, there was no good angle to hide the water and spray her. It worked once where it spooked her that she got wet with no idea of how or where, but most of the time she saw it was me and just accepted that she got wet if on the counter. One time when my roommate came home, Pasta was just hanging out on the kitchen counter. She went to pet her, but she was soaked. Confused, she was like, "Why is Pasta wet?" and from the other room I shouted, "Cause she doesn't fucking listen!" That was a losing battle for me. But my cat is really smart and, truthfully, I'm really dumb and impatient.

On a positive note, my cat was in several videos for my You-Tube web series *Apt C3* years ago. We dressed her up, made her do simple tricks like pass by a doorway over and over, or jump off a chair, pose for pictures—and we did it with treats and toys as a reward. She had a limit, about five to seven takes, but she'd be pretty game and go for treats till then, and once we learned that about her we knew we had five tries to get the take. Honestly, if I think about it, I'm about a "five takes before I get grumpy" kinda performer, too!

You also have to be patient. One trick or lesson at a time. You can't be teaching your cat to pee on the potty, not jump on the table, and fetch all at once. They sleep sixteen hours a day.

Why Cats are Assholes

They are busy. Don't fill up their schedule. They aren't trying to get into Harvard.

Grumpy Cats—a Common Temperament

Some cats never warm up. I don't know why. Maybe because they came from the streets and resent this structure and house rules. Maybe because they come from a long history of grumpy "go fuck yourself" cats. My buddy Navin got his cat, Marie, in college, and she stayed distant till the day she died. You could pet her here and there, but that was about it. I think there are a lot of people that are similar. They are just nice enough to get through the workday and life but never actually let anyone in. Doesn't make them bad people. It just makes it hard to open up, hard to connect. And grumpy cats are the same. I stayed with my friend Maria in London last year and her roommate had a cat named Bluebell. He was a big, fat, black and white cat. When he sits he looks like he comes from old money and takes pleasure in foreclosing on people's homes. He didn't like to be near me, in the same room as me, or pet, and it broke my heart. I made it my mission to get close to him the week I stayed there. I pet him once and also interviewed him about why he didn't like me, and he became known as my London cat nemesis that day. I was told he had a rough childhood and I tried not to take his distance personally, but I do feel like if we spent more time together we could grow close. Alas, I may never know.

I'll be honest: if I got a pure grump I'd keep them and take care of them but I'd have to get a bubbly cat, too. I like petting and loving on cats. I also think trust breeds trust. If your cat is distant, it's probably rooted in a deep distrust. Whether it's humans in general or you specifically I don't know. But you can be more aware of how they react to loud noises or music, open and tight spaces, being pet and where, being picked up, etc. Sometimes cats stay grumpy cause you don't listen. I always love when I go to a friend's place and I head straight to their cat and I get a report card. "He loves being pet on the head and neck and flops over unexpectedly when happy but, whatever you do, do not pet his belly. He also hisses when you don't share food so we gotta eat dinner in the bathroom."

FREQUENTLY ASKED CAT QUESTION

Question: Is there a proper way to apologize to your cat when you have to move them off your lap?

Answer: I mean, "sorry" works. I chase my cat while apologizing a lot. Usually after I accidentally step on her tail or paws. But usually I lift her up and move her off me as gently as possible, like a sleeping baby (although she always wakes up and stares at me like *what is happening . . . am I levitating?*), and I say, "I'm sorry, I have to shower. Feel free to come." Cats like to know that they have the option to join, even though they probably won't. It's how I feel about parties. I don't wanna go. I'll never go. But I wanna be invited. I like that you want me to go.

11

MY FAVORITE HOLIDAY IS CATURDAY

Cats have taken over the Internet. I have my theories. I think dog owners walk their dog daily, go to dog parks, bring their dog to outdoor restaurants, cafés, and sometimes even work, so they get to show off their pups on a daily basis. Cat owners, for the most part, have indoor cats (that only get seen by friends and family when they come over, and many of those cats can be weirded out by guests and hide) or they have outdoor cats that treat the home more like a truck stop on the highway.

"Where's Spoodles?"

"I don't know. Cruising the neighborhood or tormenting a bird. He said he'd be home for dinner."

So cat owners only really get to show off their cuteness and hilarious nature via the Internet. Posting cat pics and videos is the new . . . umm . . . well, I don't know how to finish this sentence cause I don't know trends. Just know it's cool. Everyone's doing it. #WhateverIsTrending

I would always post a picture of my cat here and there on Facebook, but it started to become almost a problem when I joined Instagram. Instagram is only for posting pictures and

111

videos, and all I was doing at the time was stand-up and being depressed at home. Stand-up isn't that interesting via photos and I wasn't leaving the house so 90 percent of the pics I took and posted were of my cat. I started to get self-conscious; it started to become my identity. I talked about cats on stage and I posted pictures of my cat online. Finally one day I decided to limit it to once a week and, of course, the day I chose was Caturday. (Also known as Saturday to "regular" people.)

But my reputation was already solidified as a cat lady. My excessive cat love was brought up at shows, podcasts, radio appearances, by other comics and fans, you name it. Also even just posting a cat picture once a week apparently is still too much to "normal" people. Plus it stopped being just my cat. I'd try to take a cool picture of any cat I saw in the wild (bodega cats, outdoor cats, cats in windows, stray cats) before they ran away or ran toward me and head butted my legs to be pet. My page became the national geographic of domesticated cats. Then I started traveling overseas for work and began taking pictures of international house cats and stray cats. Since beginning to do so, I've taken some pretty epic cat pics in Thailand, the Philippines, Japan, Italy, Switzerland, and numerous other countries.

REAL MESSAGE FROM A FAN:

Fan: Do you wanna see my cat?
Me: As long as that's not a euphemism.

I don't know who invented the term Caturday, but I'm forever grateful to them. Who knew a fake word/hashtag could bring so much joy? It started making its way into my vocabulary around five to six years ago, but I think I've been celebrating Caturday my entire life. It's nice to finally have a day just for me and my faith. All my social media bios read: "I celebrate Caturday" (mostly as a warning), but my favorite messages I've gotten from fans the last few years is: "I followed you for your comedy. I stay for the cat pics."

HOW TO CELEBRATE #CATURDAY

I treat Caturday like a weekly holiday, and how you celebrate it is your choice. I will never judge you, but here are some of the things I do every Saturday to celebrate:

- Post a cat picture on Instagram (or your social media of choice). I take my catography (made-up word/profession) very seriously and wait till Saturday to show off my latest cat pic. Note: I am a person that stops everything they are doing and will stalk a cat to take a picture; I get very *Nat Geo* about it. I get low, I get close, I make sounds to get their attention. I take hundreds of pictures to make sure I get the best shot.
  - It's an art.
  - It takes practice.
  - I've lost friends.
  - I've almost been hit by cars.
  - I'm sure I've gotten fleas.

Why Cats are Assholes

These are the risks and sacrifices one makes when they are dedicated to the holiday #caturday but, like I've said, Caturday is my religion. I was raised right.

- I usually wear something with a cat on it. Cat shirt (I own more than is socially acceptable) socks, underwear, bracelets, rings, earrings (yes I own all these things). I was on the subway one weekend a few years ago going to Brighton Beach with a few friends and was wearing this shirt my friend bought me with a tabby cat using it's paws on DJ turntables. An old woman asked me if that was my cat. I looked down and then back up and said, "Yes. She's actually at a gig right now." Because Caturday is about spreading joy and lies!
- Give my cat extra treats (cause it's their holiday, too). Think body of Christ, but tuna flavored.
- Wish people Happy Caturday like one would wish Happy Holidays. I say it to audiences I'm performing for, friends, strangers. Seats magically open up on the train. It's fun.

> Whether this is your first Caturday post or not, I'd love to see your cutie. Tag **@lizmiele** and use **#WhyCatsAreAssholes** and post a picture of your furball!

114

FREQUENTLY ASKED CAT QUESTION

Question: Should I create an Instagram account for my cat?

Answer: How else are they gonna become Insta-famous?! I'm pro cats having their own IG. You could showcase them on yours, but you and I both know that's a slippery slope if you wanna maintain friendships. Honestly, I'm pretty done following humans. Moving forward, I'm all about following animal accounts. They never talk politics and always make me smile. My very personal suggestion is if you do, do a good job. Be good at photography or hire a photographer. Everyone knows what a cat looks like, so your account should be about making your cat funny and giving them a voice, or beautiful pics of your cat that make people jealous and say passive aggressive things to their cat like, "why don't you have as many followers as grumpy cat?"

12

CRAZY CAT LADIES ARE REAL

So I'm making out with a man that invented a cat toy . . . can we just sit with that for a second? If you wanna know what that feels like, it feels like dreams come true, everybody. Feels like seven-year-old me predicted the future. It's crazy. It's so crazy that I started to realize that I'm not dating present cat toy guy. I'm dating, like, what our future could be. Cause I'm already six years ahead to where we are living on a farm, paid for by his cat toy money, just surrounded by thirty cats—all named after Kardashians. It's like a cat lady dream. I don't think it's gonna work out, though. He's super boring. I have to end it. But I don't know what the protocol is. I don't know what I'm supposed to do. I was thinking about just sending him a text message that says, "I can't keep chasing a laser that's just not there."

While I'm pro rescuing cats and having a cat family, it can become an addiction. If you don't have a tight human support group, you can find yourself going from one cat to two cats to your home being just a giant litter box. People often ask me about my cats and I tell them, "oh I only have one" and they will be like "that's weird, it feels like many." Which is also not a compliment. If you seem like someone that has a lot of cats, it's because you are posting so many pictures of your one cat

online that people, to justify this behavior, assume it's not the same cat. This feels sad. I literally made a rule that I could only post pics of my cat on Saturday for #caturday as a way of fixing my reputation (although I think the damage is done).

I have no issues with people labeling me as a woman that loves cats. I don't even mind being called a "cat lady." After all, I immediately stop in my tracks whenever I see a cat, trying to take pictures and pet it. It's true. But I think most women and admitted cat ladies worry about leveling up into "crazy cat lady" territory. We all think, *I could never. It would never happen to me*, and then one bad breakup and I'm in my bed on petfinder.com asking myself, "Why can't I adopt a litter of kittens? How does that make me anything other than a saint?"

I used to think I didn't have vices. I like sugar, but I can be reasonable about it. But every depressive bout or bad breakup I legit think, "I'm ready to start a fur family!" Whenever my feelings become too much I start trying to fill my empty heart with cuteness and fur. It's 100 percent not healthy and I fully understand how the crazy cat lady life begins.

Crazy cat ladies are real, and while they might be providing a home for lots of cats, many of the ones you read about online are often sad and toxic environments for the person living there and the cats themselves. I personally came up with a "how many cats" meter I use whenever I feel drawn to getting another that helps keep my furry compulsion in check.

SINGLE: 1–2 CATS

Like tattoos, I highly advise you wait a year before getting a second. Unless they are siblings/mother and child, then you're a good person—go right ahead and get two at once.

PARTNERED OR MARRIED: 1–3 CATS

This is a true fur family commitment. When I was dating my first real boyfriend after college a friend asked, "Is it serious?" and I said, "I mean, we have cats together. It's pretty serious."

DIVORCED: BACK DOWN TO 1–2 CATS

Clearly, if you already had three keep them—I'm not a monster. This is more for the divorced person trying to fill a hole. Don't try to build a replacement partner out of several cats.

WIDOWED: 1 CAT, 1 DOG

When you experience loss it's important to have several animals with different needs to be there for you. I recommend a dog to get you out of the house and a cat to cuddle with on the couch.

LIVE IN A SMALL APARTMENT: 1 NORMAL-SIZED CAT

Don't be a monster. If you live in a cage-sized apartment don't torture yourself and them. Only rich people can afford to have fat cats.

RANCH HOUSE: 2 CATS, TOPS

Cats, while small, need space to get away from you, your family, guests, and other animals. If you don't want your house to smell like a litter box and your cats to act like teenagers, let them have room to roam.

LARGER HOUSE: NUMBER OF BEDROOMS MINUS 1

Example: 5 bedrooms - 1 = 4 cats

There needs to always be a room or two you can hide from your cat when they are pissing you off.

OWN A FARM AND THEY MOSTLY STAY OUTSIDE: 1–5 CATS

That is unless you own large animals, then it's one cat per every two large animals. Four cows and two horses means you can have three cats.

Where did you get this math, Liz? Well, I've studied relationships, homes, interviewed thousands of pet owners . . . I made it up, but I still think I'm right. Cat hoarders have a bad rap for a reason. To provide a good living environment there needs to be balance, and most cats don't like others so either get a larger space or keep the kitty number down.

THE CAT/WITCH DUO HISTORY

As I talked about earlier in the book, cats and women share a long history of being persecuted and connected to each other. It makes sense that women who feel unseen or unheard might feel connected to another animal that has been represented in the same manner.

They believe the turning point came with the book *Malleus Maleficarum* in 1486. It was also known as the Hammer of Witches, and was almost like a guidebook on how to identify and prosecute witches during the Inquisition. The book turned society's focus on witches and classified women and cats as evil.

The Catholic Church believed cats were used by the Devil to communicate with witches and recruit young women into witchcraft. Which if true makes them *way* more hard-working than dogs (I'm just saying). I can just imagine cats outside grocery stores and schools like Army recruiters targeting young women. "Have you thought about becoming a witch? You can

make your own hours. The uniform is very slimming. Here, take a brochure. Yes, the candy is free."

So all this led to the torturing and killing of thousands of cats ordered by Pope Innocent VIII (Innocent my ass!), and this feline genocide created an excess of rodents that lead to the rampant spread of the Black Plague! WHAT ARE WE LEARNING HERE, GUYS? Anyone wanna send my book to the lawmakers in Australia that are killing thousands of cats?! This is history repeating itself!

Women and cats have been friends and accidental partners in crimes they didn't commit for thousands of years. It makes sense that they feel a kinship. This is why I think it's our duty, ladies, to protect them during this confusing time in history. (And men, you can do your part . . . this section just happened to be about cats dying due to their lady friendships.)

FREQUENTLY ASKED CAT QUESTION

Question: If a single guy has a cat, what does that mean?

Answer: It means he likes cats.

13

INDOOR/OUTDOOR CATS VS. INDOOR/OUTDOOR PEOPLE

A lot of people wonder if they should have an indoor or outdoor cat. You could look at logical info. How big is your space? How safe is your neighborhood? What does your cat prefer? Or you could look within yourself and try to shape your cat into the cat you want it to be based on your own needs. The question isn't really should my cat be indoors or outdoors, it's really are you an indoor or outdoor human?

INDOOR PEOPLE

I'm a sweatpants-all-day, eat-food-in-bed kind of person (and this was before 2020). This is who I am; it's my culture. I'm cold and lazy most of the time, don't judge me. My preferred identity is "inside person." I like being indoors, under covers and blankets. My hair looks best indoors. My skin is happiest inside. All my friends are inside. I keep my snacks inside. I can control the temperature inside. I like my roommates. I like my stuff. I don't care that my apartment is small. I'd rather watch a movie in bed on my laptop than go to the movies. Amazon Prime and food delivery are now extensions of my personality. I move

cause I have to, not cause I want to. That isn't to say I don't enjoy outdoor things, but I don't dilly dally. I do them and then I go back indoors. Every time I was at a pool party when I was a kid, this was the exchange:

"Where's Liz?"

"Inside."

Are you an indoor person? If so, then you need to talk to your cat about the benefits of being an indoor cat. It's safe, you know everyone there, there are reliable hiding spots, you can annoy humans till they feed you or pet you. They have heating pads everywhere (computer, phone, laps). You can pee and poop while being warm. You meet no one new, and that's really the point. Stranger danger was coined for you guys.

OUTDOOR PEOPLE

I know them. I've met them. I have friends that are outdoor people (we don't hang out much). I thought about being one for a few days (three, actually) because of a guy and then decided I couldn't even try to fake it. They are adventurers. Their idea of vacation is mountain climbing and camping. They are hunter/gathers (which is what I call myself when I walk five blocks to the grocery store). They prefer meeting people in person and hanging out rather than texting and dating apps. They smile for no reason. I think the sun gives them energy. They say things like, "I get stir crazy being inside too long." (What does that even mean?!) They like being in touch with nature and people. They own several backpacks that all have different purposes.

Outdoor cats often start out as outdoor cats. Sounds like a dumb statement, but what I mean is stray and feral cats grew to prefer their freedom, to come and go as they please and have confidence that they will find or catch food if not provided. They look both ways before crossing the street. They are street smart! (That's what that means, right?) They have both cat friends and cat enemies. They've met racoons and fought bears. They have some crazy stories and scars to match. Just like outdoor people, outdoor cats are more interesting, have more character, they have better Instagram accounts. They *are* better. But neither I nor my cat will ever die in a forest, and that's really comforting to us.

FREQUENTLY ASKED CAT QUESTION

Question: Can you take your cat out for a walk?

Answer: You absolutely can! There are cat leashes and harnesses, as well as cat/pet carriages if they are the curious/lazy type. They also have cat backpacks that kinda look like spaceships and sweatshirts with large kangaroo-like pouches any size cat can fit in.

Cat Leash/Harness

I tried walking my cat a few times, but she'd stay close to the building and huddle. She mostly seemed scared and I didn't wanna force it. But some cats love it and it's worth a try if you are both curious. I also don't think the leashes are all that expensive.

(continued)

125

Cat Carriage

Cat carriages (and really any pet carriage) is a look! I've seen a few carriages in NYC with cats, and truthfully: 1) they always make my day. I absolutely love seeing it and am fascinated by that cat just chilling, being pushed around often looking about, and 2) to say the owner looks eccentric is an understatement. Cat carriage people have never cared what anyone thought of them—and good for them! It's a statement, and I'm grateful to those people that go for it.

Cat Backpacks

The newest trend is cat backpacks. I think they are awesome and finally bought one (haven't used yet cause 2020 turned out to be the year everyone became an indoor cat), but further research shows some designs of this might not be best for a cat. Cat's need the ability to hide, and if it has a little window it might not cause them too much anxiety, but the ones where the whole front is clear doesn't offer them much of a safe space. Also needs to have proper ventilation if you live in a hot place, so be sure to do your research.

Cat Sweatshirt

And the cat pocket sweatshirt. Yes, I own it and it's great for walking around the apartment with

(continued)

126

a needy cat and really solves that *should I get up when my cats on my lap* issue since you can bring them with you anywhere. Your cat being able to chill there while being outside needs to be tested. I highly recommend if you try, have them on a leash or harness while in the pouch just in case they get spooked or try to bolt.

14

WHY DON'T MY FRIENDS LIKE CATS?

This is what I've learned from being single for so long, I learned that I suffer from the type of depression that leads to excessive cat ownership. It's real, and it can happen to you in your twenties. I don't think people understand that as a society, we're all just one devastation away from owning a cat. Whether you like them or not, everyone in five years will own a cat. Because you don't move to a new town and go, You know how I'm going to assimilate, I'm going to get something that doesn't leave the house. That's not how it works. It's not conscious. Something bad has to happen to you and then they kind of fall into your life. For me, I'm very sensitive. Everything hurts my feelings. So I had a bad day in college and came home with a cat. I felt good for, like, three years. It really helped. But you guys might be stronger. You might need something more. You might need like losing your job after thirty years and feeling less of a man or, like, losing a leg to diabetes—something real. And if you're no longer on board with this joke, it's because you have a job and you have both your legs. You haven't experienced real loss. Because if you're having sex, you're prone to an accident child. But if nobody's fucking you, you will have an accident cat. All it takes is one bad breakup, you're walking down the street sad, they're handing them out for free because nobody gives a fuck about cats, and now you have your best friend you may or may not remember to feed.

Why Cats are Assholes

It's confusing. You can't imagine your life without your cat(s), and when you lean over and show your friend a funny picture of your cat, their response might be, "I don't like cats."

HOW?! How is that even possible? Also, if my friend showed me a picture of their kid, it's certainly not OK for me to say, "I don't like kids." Even if it's true, I lie. Cause I'm a good person. I get so mad at that response. Not because it's unacceptable to not like an animal. I get it on some level, but when it's so prevalent of a statement like "women aren't funny" or "I don't get bubble tea," you get mad because it's from a place of acceptable ignorance rather than experience. Are women not funny, or do you have issues with your mother that you project onto all women that prevent you from seeing them as individuals? Is bubble tea any grosser or weirder of a concept than beer? You just haven't tried it cause you are scared to try new things. Do you not like cats, or did a parent not like them and you never decided for yourself? All it takes is one cat to jump into your lap and you'll change your mind so fast. It only takes one. I feel like cats are how people feel about marriage or having a good relationship. When someone tells me they don't like cats, I just say you haven't met *your* cat yet. Relationships suuuuuuuck until you find the right person. Animals just seem like charity work till you realize how much they give back to you.

Whenever someone says, "I don't like cats," now I just ask, "Oh, did you have a bad experience?" and immediately most people go, "Oh no" and give some lame non-story about an experience they didn't personally have. I'm sure this is how most snake lovers feel. I see you snake people, we aren't too far behind. Unfounded animal hate is like snakes, rats, spiders (are those animals? . . . Australian spiders are almost as big as animals, so I think that counts), and then cats. And it's sad. I've met some cool snakes, my sister had rats, spiders kill important insects and are vital to life, and cats are fucking adorable. Grow up. Make your own opinions from experiences and facts rather than cultural hate and complacency. (This goes for shitty isms, too! There's good and bad people, there's good and bad cats—don't generalize kids!)

If none of this works on friends, may I suggest the Instagram account @CashCats. It's just pics of cats with money and, sometimes, guns. It's hilarious. I show it to friends when they are sad. Fixes everything.

FREQUENTLY ASKED CAT QUESTION

Question: I'm allergic to cats (or I hate cats), so why do they like me so much?

Answer: Cats are like women. Too much attention and you repel them. I personally don't like being hit on. It makes me uncomfortable. It feels unnatural. It feels like you have an endgame as opposed to actually wanting to get to know me. I think that's why I've always related to cats. They are like, *What? You just like me cause I'm cute and soft? Fuck off, I have more value than that!* But when you are someone or some cat with a lot of value and people aren't immediately drawn to it, you get curious . . . *Oh, what do they have if they aren't interested in me?* When you are allergic

(continued)

131

or don't like cats you avoid them, don't acknowl-edge them, and it makes them crazy. It seems like you're hiding something they might want. Also, people that don't give you attention are a challenge, and cats like a good challenge—hence lasers! Cats are natural hunters, even when it comes to affection.

CONCLUSION: CAN YOU FIX AN ASSHOLE CAT?

So now you know why your cat acts the way it does and how to share a space with them, but that doesn't really help you if things aren't working out. Here are some thoughts to better all-around cohabitation with your furry devil friend.

FOOD

It's important to all of us, but it's their happiness. If you are an adult, most of us know when and how to obtain our next meal. I'm not saying money being tight might not make it stressful or less plentiful, but we all-around know when we are gonna eat because it's in our control. Cats have to wait. And who likes waiting for their favorite thing? We don't even like waiting for something we didn't even know we wanted until we saw it online. We look forward to more things than food, yet even we get annoyed when our food seems to take forever at a restaurant. So be thoughtful and consistent about feeding time. Create a schedule and habits that work for both of you. First thing I do in the morning is feed my cat (cause she's probably either being annoying about it as soon as she sees my eyes open OR she's following me around and tripping me . . . so, for safety reasons, distracting her with food is important). It doesn't have to be the

133

Why Cats are Assholes

first thing you do in the morning, but just know if food comes from the kitchen and the first thing you do is go in the kitchen, they are gonna assume you are there to feed them. So maybe, before you leave, do that so you aren't playing mind games.

If you are not home all day and your cat isn't a good food regulator (I've had both cats that can graze on dry food when hungry and it lasts for days and cats that, if I went out of town for two days and left food, they'd eat it all within the first hour), know your cat before doing this. But if they are good at self-regulating, leave some extra dry or wet food out while you're gone and then again set up a habit for dinner. Is it the first thing you do when you get home? Is it after changing? Whatever it is, again, know that if you go to the kitchen for a snack and they are hungry they are gonna be confused as to why you aren't feeding them. So if your cat is being annoying, crying, aggressive, it might be because you haven't set up a consistent food schedule.

Oh, and water. My cat sticks her head in every cup of water left anywhere. She drinks out of the toilet. Pretty much every water container but her own. Cats have learned to distrust still water, so if you want your cat to use their water bowl, clean and change regularly. Also consider putting their water dish in a different location than their food. Cats don't enjoy the scent of food while drinking and food particles in their water, and cat behaviorists believe this comes from cats hunting away from water sources in the wild as to not contaminate it. Your cat isn't annoying, it's smart!

PLAYTIME

Some cats are more active than others. Kittens clearly have a lot of energy, but some cats—up into their teens—are still jumping around. Yes they sleep a lot, but every animal needs some activity. Some cats need you to play with them, some can entertain themselves or respond well to self-regulating toys, and some are busy hunting the roaches and mice you didn't even know you had! All this said, playtime is important and can be fun for both of you. For me, playtime often starts cause Pasta attacks my sweatshirt string or confuses my feet under the covers with a mouse. So I'll start playing with her based off her already being in a playful mood and maybe it inspires me to find her little mice or get the feather stick. Sometimes it starts cause I trip over her bell ball and it flies across the room and she gets excited. Other times she's being aggressively cuddly when I have shit to do and, like a dog, I throw a ball halfway across the room just to have some alone time. However, playtime starts and however long it lasts isn't as important as it being a ritual you guys share.

NAPTIME

I'm sure you'd be pissed if someone disturbed your naptime, and you might being thinking, "This lazy bastard sleeps all day! It's not a big deal if I'm annoying." But it is. You are breaking their trust. Just like you'd be angry if your roommate, sibling, friend, spouse jostled you awake for no goddamn reason. It's the same thing. I'm not saying you need to tip toe around your cat or not live your life, although I love how crazy that would be. You are home and a friend calls and you're like, "Hey, sorry. I can't talk. My cat's sleeping." Sleeping is one of our most vulnerable times, and while cats are light sleepers and seem to wake up easily, there's no real reason to bother them while sleeping unless they are on your stuff or you need to bring them somewhere. So if your cat is hiding, runs away when you come into the room, or isn't being nice to you, you might wanna look at what kind of behavior you or the people in your house are doing when your cat is trying to sleep. Same can be said for leaving them alone when they eat or go to the bathroom. All three are important and vulnerable times when no one wants to be fucked with. Be a good friend and cat owner. Leave them be.

ALONE TIME/FREEDOM

I think cats are natural introverts. Well, not all cats. I think some are more social than we give them credit for, but most seem to do better alone than maybe dogs or people. In general, as someone that does better when they have more alone time than social time in the day, I think cats cherish it and are healthiest when they can go about their day as they please. If you guys just so happen to meet on the couch or while both walking to the kitchen, cool. Say hi, ask about each other's day, but forcing your cat to be your home companion 24/7 is aggressive. If your cat isn't behaving in a kind way it might be because you are asking too much of them. If you want someone to obey every word and follow you around like a puppy . . . well, then get a puppy. I think cats are less work all around but also less attentive—and that's a compromise you make. All cats are different, and those that are distant in the beginning can soften and become cuddle bugs. My cat is a true testament of this but, as Albert Einstein once wrote: "Everybody is a genius. But if you

136

judge a fish by its ability to climb a tree, it will live its whole life believing that it is stupid." If you keep trying to force a cat to be a dog, you will both feel misunderstood and angry.

SNUGGLE TIME

All that said, you will know when your cat wants to snuggle. They rub up against your leg, crawl into your lap, butt their head into you, sometimes they bite, pull your hand onto them. If it's considered sexual assault, it's kinda exactly what a cat does to show it wants attention.

Most of us like being touched, and cats kinda have a bad rap that they are aloof, unloving, and bitey, but when your cat asks for petting or snuggles, take a few minutes to show them love. This is how you build a loving and affectionate relationship. If you ignore them or are shitty then they will eventually stop asking. These relationships—and all relationships in general—are not always convenient, but if you want someone (or your cat) to be there when you want them to, it's worth taking the time to show up for them and be there for them when they want love. You don't have to leave the house or go to anyone's baseball game. Just pet them, snuggle with them, brush them, hold them when they ask.

FRIENDSHIP

I love and am very jealous of those videos that go viral of a hot guy (it's always a hot guy) with a cat on his shoulder as he rides a bike or he's on the beach and his cat follows him everywhere. If I'm being honest, while I don't hike with my cat and we don't have any viral videos together (YET!), we do have a unique and beautiful friendship that we built over time. It's special to me, and I'm sure it looks special to people looking from the outside. My cat has been there for me during sooo many breakups, depressive episodes, times where I had no money, times where I've had some money and then back to no money. She's treated me the same no matter how big my career has gotten or how many opportunities didn't work out. The best thing about pet friendship is they accept you as you are. Not what you hope to be or what you are working toward, who you'll be when you lose weight, get that job, get a better house, or after years of therapy. It's the purest of friendships. They love you now, as you are. It's to your advantage to accept them and love them as *they* are. And let them teach you about real love.

SO, TO RECAP: WHY IS MY CAT AN ASSHOLE?

Because they are not being treated like the god/goddess they know they are.

Thanks for reading. Now please be sure to leave this out so that your cat can enjoy it, too!

(Or use it as a bed.)

138

FACQ: (FREQUENTLY ASKED CAT QUESTIONS)

When I was working on this book, I asked my fans online if there were any burning questions they wanted answered about cats. I was blown away by the response, and honestly some questions were so funny I couldn't *not* include. Here are some frequently asked cat questions and my best possible answers.

Q: Do my two adopted cats think they are brother and sister, or do they believe they've been forced into a diabolical, sexless arranged marriage since both are neutered/spayed?

A: I don't know. Have you ever sat them down to talk about this arrangement? I know my siblings are my siblings because my parents told me they were every day and because I hate them (joking). Any confusion really sounds like a lack of openness in your household, and you need to set them straight! But if I'm being honest, if they are neutered/spayed then they aren't thinking about sex. They are thinking, *Why is this asshole in my house leaving his fur everywhere?*

139

Q: Can cats recognize their own face in the mirror?
A: They can't. They think it's another cat. Very few animals recognize themselves in the mirror, so your cat isn't vain or they don't hate themselves. They think it's an intruder. I think the best thing you can do is teach your cat to be nice to other cats so they doesn't try to attack and break your mirror. That's seven years of bad luck for you and one year of bad luck for them.

Q: Do cats just pretend not to know the word "no?"
A: Yes.

Q: Who invented the laser pointer for cats?
A: I don't know if this has a full answer. Someone invented the laser pointer and I can only assume some scientist or professor owned a cat and was practicing giving a talk with it at home and their cat went nuts. And as everyone knows, working and preparing are boring and so they started using it to play with their cat. Then the next day at work it was their little anecdote to seem relatable and fun to their students. They were like, "Funny story. I was practicing my lesson plan last night using the laser pointer and my cat went nuts chasing it. How fun is that?" Then some girl that's pretty sure she's gonna drop out of his class cause science isn't her passion (her parents just pressured her)

140

gets curious, so she goes home and buys one. (I don't know how. I honestly don't remember how people found stuff before the Internet and Amazon). Then she starts playing with her cat who goes fucking nuts! And she thinks, *I could sell these. I could be a cat toy mogul.* And that's what she did, and her parents accepted it because she bought them a house with cat laser money and that's all parents care about. (This is all made up but I don't think I'm far off, so I stand by it.)

Q: Once my cat has fallen asleep on my lap, what's the acceptable amount of time to remain stationary before I can live my life again?
A: This is a great question I've struggled with myself. As my cat is bitey/an asshole, I have three rules that make when I do move her easier, which may help.

1. If I'm doing something stationary and she's sleeping and not in the way of my view or getting work done, she's allowed to stay there till right before I'm about to pee my pants. I'll not eat and accept getting muscle cramps. Whatever. If you are like a lap paper weight, I respect your work and will not disturb you. Often times, as a writer, she has helped keep me at my desk and focused on the task at hand and, for that, I'm grateful. Other times I've missed two meals and felt disconnected to the outside world, and

that's her fault. I'd miss my own wedding if my cat sat on my lap right before I had to leave for the ceremony.

2. If you bite me, all contractual obligations of not moving are off. The spell of liking you is broken once you bite me. We've known each other too long, and me reaching over to get something or moving your leg cause it's stabbing my vagina are legit reasons, and violence will not be tolerated. So once a cat hisses, bites, or scratches, I push them off my lap and go about my life and we have a timeout. Sometimes she jumps back up immediately and I'll let her resettle if she seems to have gotten the message, but 90 percent of the time she goes and finds a corner and calls me a "bitch" under her breath, and that's fine.

3. If the cat is in the way, you have somewhere to be (e.g., a job), or you can't feel your legs, I think five to ten minutes of snuggles is respectable. Then I usually scooch her over to a position that is more suitable for me, or place her somewhere and head out. More often than not I abandon plans and friends until she decides she's done with me. But I have moments of self-esteem and respect and I let her know. She is always shocked, as if I'm a plant that's come to life and vomited on her.

142

Q: Do cats have egos?
A: Yes, they certainly do. If cats ran their own Instagram accounts they'd all say "model" in the bio. They all think they are the best. Some of this has to do with the solitary lifestyle they partake in. My cat was an only cat most of her life and the few cats she did meet were kittens. She's always thought she was the smartest, biggest cat in the room—and she wasn't wrong. But like a child that's only been told "you're amazing" from their parents, I think this often-unfounded praise can have consequences. It's your responsibility to talk to your cat about being a good person (cat).

Q: Are dumb cats better than smart cats?
A: How do you define *better*? The problem with smart cats is they know what they are doing. My cat waits for me to turn my back to steal chicken off my plate. Dumb cats do it in front of you. Same behavior. Neither will stop, no matter the consequences. So the real question is: Do you want a cat that lies to you, or a cat that tells the truth? Honestly, both are funny so I feel like it's a win-win. My cat is really smart yet still gets her head stuck in a Pringles can. Maybe all cats are a mix and we just choose to see what we wanna see.

Q: How do I know if my cat is depressed?

A: This is a real thing. When my cat was three I moved from a decent-sized two bedroom (for NYC standards) to a tiny studio apartment (livable for almost no one's standards). I know because my cat went from having space to run and play to barely space to walk. One side of my bed touched my fridge, which touched my sink/stove, which touched my bathroom, and the other side touched my desk, which touched my door. Fun part for her is she could jump from my bed to the fridge to the cabinets and look over my entire apartment. But, I think, she hung out up there cause there really wasn't much else to do or anywhere to go. She never really played. She seemed like she was moping around. She slept more than usual. It was a hard adjustment for her and it took me time to realize, this set-up depressed me as well. Difference is I could leave the house. She was depressed with the move for about six months, but she finally adjusted and after getting bed bugs (it was a real great apartment as you can see!) I threw a lot of stuff out, which freed up some room.

Point is, if your cat is eating less, playing less, hiding more, sleeping more, it's a sign that they could be either depressed or it could be a serious sign of illness. Any major change in behavior should be taken seriously and they should be taken to the vet. If nothing physical is wrong, take a moment to think over any changes to their life that might be bumming them out. Did you move? Did you get a new roommate? Have a baby and now don't play with them? Get busy at work

144

and leave them home alone a lot more? Go on vacation? Start seeing a new person? Stop seeing an old person? Cats have feelings, even though you can't see them in their face. They might need a hug, pep talk, some playtime, or extra love. Like you'd check in and be there for a friend going through a rough time, you should do the same with your cat!

Q: Do cats have superpowers?
A: Honestly, it's hard to think they don't. Their eyes look like laser beams in light, they can jump crazy distances like Spider-Man. They are even self-cleaning! I think cats are extraordinary, and their talents are only limited by their drive. I bet if they didn't sleep and get distracted by string and bugs so much they'd have gathered a kitty Avengers crew by now. I call movie rights on *Kitty Avengers*.

Q: Do cats know of Garfield?
A: Garfield is like one of the first cat celebrities. Maybe the new Gen X cats don't know of them cause they are uncultured, but I truly think all cats know and respect Garfield and what he has done to bring awareness to the importance of napping, creating personal space from humans and dogs, and the dangers of eating too many carbs before bed.

Q: How often should I play with my cat?

A: Every cat is different. Some cats entertain themselves pretty efficiently and you can just join in randomly when you have time. Others need a lot of attention or some encouragement—especially if it's leading to a weight problem, which can lead to health issues and a shorter lifespan. Also, kittens, like kids, have a lot of energy and will wanna play more, while older cats will most likely have less energy and wanna be left alone to watch Netflix by themselves. Your cat will let you know how much playtime it needs.

Q: Are some cats narcissistic?

A: A narcissist, by definition, is "a person who has an excessive interest in or admiration of themselves." I don't think cats really care about themselves that much. If we were gonna diagnose a mental illness on cats, I'd think they are more depressed than narcissistic. I actually think cats by nature are pretty indifferent in how they think about themselves. There is something really noble and punk rock about how you feed them and take care of them and they don't suck up at all. They join you when they want. They don't when they don't want to. I feel like cats have healthy self-esteem and boundaries, and when you don't have your own it can come off as selfish (says the woman trying to learn how to set her own healthy boundaries).

Q: How much do cats shed?
A: Shedding is completely normal. Cats shed some fur every day and also go through one or two big sheds and fur growth cycles per year. I think I shed more than my cat does. Shedding can be somewhat contained by brushing their fur or dressing in the same color as your cat so that you never know if you have cat hair on you. It's why I wear all black. :)

Q: My cat no longer likes my live-in girlfriend. How do I rehome a middle-aged woman?
A: Great question. There are tons of shelters that would take in any middle-aged women. It's always a shame when we feel you've provided a forever home for a woman—especially when they are in their later years—and it doesn't work out. That's life. You can help them find temporary living with many of the home/apartment-finding sites. Craigslist if you don't care about them, Apartments.com if you do. Maybe you might have friends that would take her in. Relocating a woman when its creating a hostile living environment is important to you and your cat's safety.

147

Q: Why does my cat keep putting their butt in my face?

A: I think the real question is, why don't you put your butt in *their* face? It's actually a nice thing what they're doing. Cats put their butt in your face for a few reasons.

- As a hello. We learned as humans to wave, shake hands, or hug as a friendly greeting, but cat parents taught them to present their butt. Different cultures. Different traditions. You bow in China. You show your butt to a cat. Be respectful!
- Letting you know they aren't a threat. We would tell people, "Hey, I come in peace," but they don't have that ability so they show their backside as a way of being like, "Hey, you can trust me."
- A way of showing friendship and trust. Again, it's their hug.
- A cat's main scent comes from here, so it's just a way of helping you get to know them. My favorite perfume is "Honeysuckle" by Fresh, and I also wear Trader Joe's coconut lotion every day (it's really good!). While I can't really smell me, I know that's my scent. I like to think it's a kind and inviting scent, just like cats like to think their butt scent is kind and inviting.

148

Q: Do cats stop recognizing their owners if they haven't seen them in a while?

A: Cat's actually don't have the best facial recognition, but they do recognize their owners; it might just be from other variables. Scent, sound of voice, the way we feel, etc. I left my cat with my mom for two years (visiting maybe once every other month) and was worried she'd stop recognizing me and be mad at me, but during visits she was kinda indifferent and when I finally brought her home last year it took maybe half a day but she was right back to being the needy "I need to be with you all the time" kitty she was before I dropped her off.

Q: How many cats should I have when I die so that they will completely devour my corpse?

A: Way to be ecofriendly! I've long believed burial is a waste of money, resources, and space. I've always planned on being cremated but as new innovation with cremation is coming along (did you know your ashes can be turned into a plant?), I'm trying to think of more and more ways my body can give back. And maybe it's by providing a meal for your kitty friends. If I were you I'd pay attention to your cat's eating habits. My cat has always been a light eater but my ex-boyfriend's cat, Humphrey, was a big boy that would eat all day if we allowed him. Plus you have to factor in your size. I'm the size of a middle schooler so my

guess for these two eater types is: Three Humphreys and Two Pastas. For bigger people I'd give or take a Humphrey.

Q: Why do cats bury their poop?
A: Cats pee and poop on stuff to mark their territory. Smaller cats—like your house cat—often buries its poop as a way of ensuring that the dominant cats do not feel challenged. If you don't live with another cat, I think that dominant cat is you. My cat wouldn't bury her poop when I first got her and it smelled up my tiny apartment, so when she was a kitten after she pooped we'd go over as a family and I'd take her little paw and help her bury her poop (the same way you might teach a kid how to wipe or flush the toilet). I don't know if she grew as a kitty or caught on or was tired of being yelled at, but she is an adult woman cat that now buries her poop and everyone is proud!

Q: What can cats do about climate change?
A: I'm sure litter is super wasteful and unhelpful to keeping the earth clean. That's where dogs pooping outside is kinda ideal (although the plastic bags people pick them up is less so). It's all so hard! It think discussing with your cat about finishing all its food and

150

not just the food in the middle of the bowl is helpful to being less wasteful. Maybe showing interest in their toys for more than a day would also cut down on waste. It's hard. How do you tell a cat that the world is ending when they don't leave the house?

Q: What is my cat hiding?
A: You know the other day when you put down a pen on your desk and then went back and swore you put it there but it wasn't? Or you were holding ten dollars to run and get some eggs but then when you looked for it in your pocket you couldn't find it? Or you were braiding your hair and you reached for a hair tie and you couldn't find any? That's all your cat. Your cat is a pickpocket meets ninja meets your elementary school bully. They want whatever you have cause they understand it has value . . . then they hide it all in a secret location. It's like a treasure chest (but with more hair), and they stockpile what they believe to be your most valuable possessions. It's why they are always sleeping on your computer or under your car. They are trying to steal it, but it's too heavy. So they take all your small treasures hoping to someday trade it in to the cat black market, better known as the "Black Cat Market." Some cats are better at hiding their treasures than others. If you find your cat's stash, it's cause they are dumb or that is their decoy stash to throw you off. If you don't find their stash, it's cause you are dumb.

151

Q: If a cat sees a big cat (e.g., lion, tiger, cheetah) on TV, do they get jealous?

A: As a small person that is always surrounded by bigger, stronger people (male or female), I don't really get jealous that they are so much bigger than me as I just get curious about their giant life. I don't think cats think they are missing out cause they aren't huge—especially seeing as there are a lot of benefits to being small. I think they are just kinda mesmerized that there is an option to get that big and wonder if they are just in the caterpillar stage of their someday butterfly life. I think most cats believe they are a multivitamin and a growth spurt away from becoming tiger sized. At least that's what I've always hoped for myself.

Q: Why are cats always in a cuddle mood when you are about to leave and don't have time?

A: Cats seem to like you best when you aren't interested. It's a toxic love thing. Some people like to chase love cause that's how they grew up. So cats seem to be most drawn to people and want attention when it's not readily available. The way some people like jewelry or fashion solely based on its scarcity. When love is scarce, they become affectionate. It's not right, it's frustrating, but its why most people are late to work and dinner. Understand that it's not them, it's their inconsiderate, controlling cat.

152

Q: Does my cat like me?

A: I dunno. How are they behaving toward you? If they are butting their head against you, purring when you pet them or hold them, greeting you, or just pleasantly indifferent to you then, yeah, they do. If they run away every time you are in the room, hide, hiss when you get close, don't let you near or touch them, try to scratch out your eyes, I think they aren't a fan. Not saying it doesn't take cats time to warm up to you (give it time if they are new to your home) or that they don't have bad days (we all do, bro, I hissed at four people last week!), but indifference or wanting to be near you—if even for five seconds—is big.

Q: The furball. True health issue or just more fucking drama?

A: Furballs are natural. They clean themselves and then they get rid of the excess fur. Think of it like when you clean out your hairbrush or a vacuum, but it's wet and ruins your sheets. Best way to maybe help them is to brush them and catch some of the excess fur before they do. But this is natural. Now where they throw up is pure aggression and hostility toward you and everything you love.

153

Q: Does having a cat count as having a kid?

A: What's your definition of a kid? If you are having a kid for the right reasons, then probably not. But if you would have a kid for the wrong reasons—you wanna feel loved, less lonely, never want them to leave, they have to hang out with you, you wanna take care of something—then yeah, cats are the best kind of kid cause you can emotionally scar them and because they can't talk or start a blog or become a stand-up comic, no one will know. Cats are kids that never go to college and I honestly think some parents didn't realize that's what they really wanted. Instead of growing up, maybe the best thing to do for your abandonment issues is find an animal that can't abandon you! (I'm sure this is the wrong answer.) All I'm saying is kids are expensive, a lot of work, you can (and probably will) do it wrong, then they leave and don't call enough. Your mom thinks you should have kids but she needs to prove herself as a grandma and start pulling her weight with the furbabies first. Tell her they will also need twenty dollars for Christmas!

Q: Have you ever dreamt of being a cat?

A: Most days. I love sleeping, I care about my hair, I have big eyes, I speak my mind but I'm also pretty easy to get along with. I think I'd make a good cat and, truthfully, I think I could use the rest.

Q: Why does my cat hate my slippers so much?
A: Your slippers sound old and racist. Get new slippers!

Q: Does my cat watch me when I sleep?
A: Probably. Ninety percent of the time I wake up and my cat is staring at me, either up close or from across the room. I don't know if her kitty senses are so good that she can hear or feel me stirring in my sheets or if she's been perched at my feet all night waiting for me to wake up and feed her, but it is always off-putting. No one likes feeling eyes on them. It's uncomfortable. It feels creepy, even when you love someone. I think there is some concern involved. Almost like a roommate wondering why you haven't left for work yet on a Tuesday morning and not knowing if they should wake you. Or they are staring as a way of watching over you. Not because they care about you, per se, but they care about the literal hand that feeds them. The same way you might make sure you fully wash and dry a can opener so it doesn't rust. You care for it because it does helpful stuff for you. Or perhaps it's just curiosity. Like I've watched my cat sleep through jack hammering right outside our window, yet if I drop a vitamin from the other room she wakes up and runs over to see if it's a treat.

155

Q: Do cats wanna kill the red dot or be its friend?
A: I think cats are just super curious. I don't know if they wanna kill it necessarily as much as they wanna find out what the fuck it is. Do you know how many times my cat has caught a bug or a mouse then looked at it, poked it, stared at it, and then just let it slowly walk away? I think they wanna catch it and figure out what it is and how much work it will be to eat it. How is their red dot or bug-hunting any different than fishing as a pastime? They are catching and releasing. We are just upset because it's in our home. Cats are just old men bug-fishing.

Q: My cat watches me shower. Perv, or worried I'm gonna drown?
A: Aw man, this is *the* question! In my second apartment in NYC you could go up to the roof. Nothing special about it. You just had access, and I'd bring beach chairs up there in the summer and just chill and drink beers with friends. One night we go up there and there's a guy and he looks at us, looks across to the building next to ours and then looks down disappointed and leaves. It was really weird. So then we look across at the other building and it's someone showering behind frosted glass, but it was a very clear silhouette of a woman. We busted out laughing. If that were my cat she would not have left. Pervs feel shame, cats don't. Maybe it's because they bathe in front of people

all the time and it's not a big deal to them. They are just staring, wondering who is spitting on us.

In my old apartment Pasta would walk between the clear curtain and the regular shower curtain and pace, but in my new apartment I have a stand-up shower with a frosted door and she sits on the end of the sink and stares. I'd like to think she's equal parts curious and concerned. She HATES water and I think she sees me as brave/stupid the way we all do when someone skydives for fun. My cat is such a creepy starer that I kept telling myself even if she was being creepy at least she's a girl cat and we technically have the same parts. I just look like a fully shaved version of her. I think most cat's minds are truly curious and every day they are like, *wow ... this form of bathing seems wasteful and wildly inefficient . . .* and they aren't wrong. So my final answer is cats can't be pervs. They are more like species tourists just trying to understand our ways.

Q: How is sleeping in that position comfortable?
A: The Internet is full of pictures and videos of cats sleeping in the weirdest positions. My cat sleeps on piles of shoes. How is that comfortable? I've seen cats sleep on their backs like starfish, like a loaf but their head is face down on the bed, with their head hanging off the edge, asleep on the skinniest of ledges/top of doors. I think at the end of the day we have to remember that cats are professional sleepers. They spend

over half their day sleeping. They are just more effi-cient, and better at it than we are. My dad is no differ-ent. He can sleep in any chair, sometimes standing up, while driving. He's a pro. If you trained hard like them maybe you could sleep on a railing too!

Q: Does my cat understand me?
A: Do they understand words, or do you mean do they understand your nature and needs?

Do they understand words?

Technically, they do. Not as many as dogs. They say dogs can recognize up to a hundred words, while cats are more in the twenty-five- to thirty-five-word range. But they respond to inflection and cadence more than the words themselves, and respond to words they hear frequently. Cats know the difference between angry and friendly tones, so don't let them fool you. Repeat-ing words with the same tone is important.

Do they understand me as a person?

I believe they think we are silly and cute the same way we think they are silly and cute. I bet they see us star-ing at the computer or TV for hours and think, *What the fuck are they looking at?* If they had social media they'd

take a pic and post, "My human has been staring at this black box for hours. What a weirdo!" I bet they think we are gross cause they never see us licking ourselves. I'm sure they wonder how their vegetarian owners survive without meat. I'm sure they think we would be more fun to play with if we slept more than eight hours a day.

Q: Would cats need us if they had opposable thumbs?
A: No. If I'm being honest, they don't need us now. I think they are just lazy/smart. Why do something yourself when someone will do it for you? Cats are very self-sufficient. First, they are predator animals so they aren't like helpless gerbils, and secondly they don't need much. Food. Water. Maybe warmth. Opposable thumbs would just make them more mischievous and annoying. Imagine them picking up your stuff and then dropping it, as opposed to just knocking it down? That's cats with thumbs.

Q: Why do all cats only allow three belly rubs before they attack?
A: So some cats like it, but I've only really been around cats that hate it. Theory is that their sensitive organs are located near their underbellies and it's a protec-

tive instinct. Which is confusing because they show their belly as a sign of trust. But you know pretty quickly if they don't like it, so if they don't, don't do it. Might make you sad cause it's like the softest part, but I don't let strangers touch my butt and I bite back on that pretty hard, too. Be respectful. Don't #metoo your cat.

Q: Does catnip make cats high?
A: Yes! You are essentially dosing them with a psychoactive drug. It's 100 percent weed for cats. Bet some

of you didn't realize you were so liberal. Cats have had more rights than humans for years! Difference is humans respond differently to weed, while all cats affected by catnip essentially react the same way. They roll around, salivate, eat it, and at times fight with other cats (kinda sounds more like our alcohol response). Also, about 20 to 30 percent of cats are immune and have no response to it at all. Many believe it's a genetic trait passed down, especially since lions and tigers do respond to catnip! So yeah, you are giving your cat drugs . . . but who cares? I mean, they aren't driving. They don't have a job. They don't have bills. Let them chill, brah!

Q: Should my cat have a will or godparent in case I die first?
A: Yes! I used to tell my roommate before every trip, "If I die, she's yours" and she would say "of course" and then I'd turn to Pasta and say, "Don't talk back, Carmen's in charge." Pasta had at least three people lined up that would take her in case I died. How traumatizing. I die and she's homeless. You should absolutely set something up with a friend or family member. It doesn't have to be in writing, but there needs to be a plan. I don't wanna have to be a ghost cause I didn't think ahead of time to set up a care system for my cat.

Q: Is dressing your cat up considered animal cruelty?
A: Only if they look bad. I'm sorry, if a cat can rock it, are you not taking the cat to a new status? If you post a picture and it goes viral, has the Internet not spoken and shown that your cat is a star? I'm so pro cat in hats you could call me Dr. Seuss. If the cat hates it then, yeah, don't. That's just mean. But if he/she is indifferent then what's the harm? I'm pro babies dressing as animals and cats dressed as insects and tacos and sheriffs. Why else have an animal if you can't dress it up?! Don't take this away from me. I have nothing. Sorry. My kitty is incredibly indifferent and that's half the fun. Her non-smiling face dressed up as pizza is the reason I'm happy most days. (Check her out on my IG.)

Q: How do I know if my cat is meant for fame?
A: The best rule of thumb is: If your cat was a kid, would it be bullied? Do they have a unique fur pattern? Do they have weird habits? Like, do they like to bathe in sinks? Do they try to fit in boxes a quarter their size? Do they sleep in weird positions? Do they look like other animals? Do they have a funny face? The weirder the better. All you need is a good name and a meme-maker app on your phone and you are golden. But it's work. People need to know and see your cat for them to become a sensation, so it's not just hilarious or cute content—you need to be your cat's

personal PR agent. Are you ready to put in the work to make your kitty the next Lil Bub?

Q: How do I monetize my cat?

A: Cats have mooched off their owners for too long. It's time they get a job. If butt models on Instagram can make money off one body part, your cat can surely make some dough off its furry body. The Internet is now where cat careers are taking off, from Grumpy Cat to Cinder-Block (the fat kitty that didn't want to get on the water treadmill and uses one paw). After your kitty has the followers, next is the merchandise. If people aren't wearing your kitty's face on their shirts, how will new people learn about their feline wisdom? I'm a huge Grumpy Cat fan, and my fandom accelerated when I started owning her stuff and people started purchasing kitty stuff for me. Do I need it? No. Does it enhance my life to new cat-loving levels? Hell yeah! Cat shirts, key chains, art, stickers, socks, dolls. I'm a thirty-five-year-old woman, but I still shop like a nine-year-old. My niece and I both got stickers for our birthdays and shared the same level of excitement. Don't shame me, I just love stickers! (And those who don't are liars.)

Q: Can I throw my cat a birthday party?
A: In the words of Jonathan Van Ness, "Yes, Honey!" Of course you can, and maybe that's been the key to your lack of connection over the years. Does it feel like your cat's ignoring you? Well, how many birthdays have you missed? It's all starting to make sense now, isn't it? How you celebrate is a discussion you need to have together. Does your cat like toys? Do they want extra tuna?

Now, have I thrown my cat a birthday party? Yes and no. I have bought her toys. I have dressed her up in what I decided was a respectable birthday sweater (her birthday is in May . . . it was cruel). I have canceled plans with friends to be with her. I have taken "birthday pictures." My roommates and I have been extra nice to her and wished her a happy birthday with full expectancy that she'd say thank you and offer us cake. I have felt slighted when close friends have not reached out to wish her a happy birthday . . . I've gotten just shy of sending out invites and dressing her up in a tiara.

All that said, you know your cat better than I do. If they aren't the birthday celebrating type, then just a head nod and some extra treats will do.

Q: Why is it so hard to pill cats? Do they wanna die?
A: My cat had cancer a few years ago (she's in remission and doing great, thanks for asking!), but my mom put her on chemo which was in pill form and I

164

had to give it to her three times a week. As the daughter of a vet I'd like to first say my pilling success rate is about 65 percent, and I feel really good about that cause my cat is a beast to pill. It started off easy. Those pill pockets were awesome. I'd put the pill in the treat hole, she'd eat it. Done. Then after around two weeks the fucker started eating *around* the pill! WHAT? Ten points for creativity, but zero points for taking your "staying alive" meds. So then I had to go back to prying open her mouth, throwing the pill down her throat, holding her mouth shut like she's an alligator, and then rubbing her throat to initiate swallowing. And all those moves would work most of the time, but a good 35 percent of the time she'd either spit up the pill right away or walk away and find a hiding place to spit it up. I can't even begin to tell you how many times my roommate found me on the floor of our kitchen with my cat in between my legs like we were in a wrestling match with several wet pills surrounding us and me yelling, "Do you wanna fucking die, Pasta?! Cause if the cancer doesn't kill you then I will!" Pilling my cat is number three on my list of things that have made me so mad I want to commit murder. It's:

1. Wireless printer issues (and really any technology).
2. Merging in any major cities where people speed. up when they see you coming (I'm talking to you NYC, DC, and LA . . . you're all monsters!).
3. Pilling my cat.

4. Talking to a customer service robot that keeps getting my words wrong and then won't transfer me when I start screaming OPERATOR!

5. Anything that unexpectedly breaks my nails (overhead luggage compartments, really hard-to-open shampoo bottles, drawers that are hard to open, etc.).

FALQ: (FREQUENTLY ASKED LIZ QUESTIONS)

Question: Where is Pasta now?

Answer: She is back in Brooklyn living with me. Because of the pandemic I stopped touring and was home more than I'd been in years and finally had the time to be a good cat mom again. For about two years she lived at my mom's cat clinic in New Jersey. I used to drop her off there for any work trip that was longer than four days, but then my long trips started getting longer and longer and I was away more days than I was home and it became unfair to my cat and my roommates. So for two years she roamed free in a huge animal hospital as opposed to only having a Brooklyn apartment. She was doted on by dozens of employees that loved her (Barb, Kerri, and Gwyn being some of her biggest fans). She got fat from all the different types of food at her disposal and her constant begging. She's now an old lady (fifteen years old!) and is on arthritis meds (liquid form, thank god) and living a happy cat life asleep on my lap as I type this.

167

Q: Do you really love cats as much as you say?

A: I mean, I wrote an entire book about them! If we're dating and you asked me if I really loved you and then I wrote a book about our love, that would be beyond sweet . . . and a huge red flag. I really do. I know it's cliché in some ways to be this woman who loves cats, but I was raised by veterinarians. I lived next to their clinic. I didn't have a lot of human friends growing up. Even in my thirties they make me happy. I get the same level of excitement that a seven-year-old does when they see a cat. I try to touch every cat I come across. I too am puzzled with this reaction considering all I know and how many bad experiences I have had with cats, yet I still get giddy. I can't tell you how many days my boyfriend will ask how my day was and my first response will be, "Look at this cat I met!" and then show him nine hundred pictures of an ordinary cat sleeping. I have more pictures on my phone of stray cats than I do of my friends and family. It's not healthy, but it makes me happy . . . and if I'm not hurting anyone, I think.

Q: Do you like dogs?

A: Yes! Of course. Love dogs. I'd actually really like to get a dog, but they are even harder to have than cats when you travel. Although I do have fantasies of getting famous and traveling with my dog like Adam Sandler or some other comics I know. They are a little easier to travel with than cats. It's that "I shit outside"

luxury they have. I'm just a big animal lover. I think they are all cool, fascinating, and pretty. But, if I'm being honest, I'm really lazy and think I'm more drawn to low maintenance, do-their-own-thing types of animals. Hence, cats. But hey, bring on the dog/non-cat pics! I welcome them all.

Q: How many jokes about cats do you have in your comedy act?
A: Hahaha, I have no idea. As a comic I turn over my material every two to three years, so I have cat jokes on my first and second album I don't do anymore live. In total I have released three hours of material, and the first two had a lot of cat jokes. This third hour I think I only have three, but I think because they are such a part of my life (and the only thing I actually know anything about), they will always be a part of my act in some capacity.

Q: Does Pasta like your comedy?
A: I'd like to think she is my biggest fan. I talk to myself a lot and also rehearse bits in my room, and whenever a joke used to bomb onstage I'd say, "well my cat liked it." I don't know if that's true, but I always loved how I'd be pacing in my room rehearsing or working out an idea and she would sit at the edge of my desk and

169

just stare and, sometimes, all you need as a performer is an attentive audience and she's been that for me most of my career (as well as the inspiration/butt of so many jokes). I am truly grateful for her presence and support!

PASTA'S *REAL* FAVORITE COMIC

My old roommate and one of my best friends is a brilliant comic named Carmen Lynch and has done many late-night sets where both Pasta and I have been referenced, so I actually think she might be a bigger Carmen Lynch comedy fan. (Google "Carmen Lynch Colbert" and "Carmen Lynch Conan" to hear some of her Pasta jokes.)

Q: If either you or your cat could be famous, who would you choose?

A: I mean, let's be honest. She has two established comedians joking about her. Pasta feels pretty famous. She also has a Facebook fan page Carmen made that neither of us maintain (gotta hate poor management). But that's a hard question. I think my cat. I actually don't need the limelight and really love creating and filtering my ideas through others. When I used to make my weekly web series with my roommates Carmen Lynch and Chris Vongsawat called *Apt C3*, we were kinda a

cast of four. It was us and Pasta. We took weekly funny pictures with all four of us and did many sketches that centered on or involved Pasta. I loved creating content around her, figuring out how to get her to do stuff (or at least look like she was doing certain stuff on camera), and I loved all the praise she got. I was very much headed toward being a stage mom and I think I'm more comfortable and confident when I promote something one degree away from myself. I don't know if it's low self-esteem or just not wanting that much attention, but I looked at Grumpy Cat's life and always thought I'd love that for me and Pasta. She deserves to be on merchandise! (I did sell T-shirts that an artist friend designed based on a picture of her years ago, so she kinda did for a moment in time.) She is beloved, though. I've had a few shows over the years where people yell out her name when I mention my cat in passing and it warms my heart. I have zero doubts that if she had a better manager she would have made it big!

Q: Do you regret not becoming a veterinarian like your parents?
A: Yes and no. Yes because I think I would have really enjoyed being around animals all day long and probably wouldn't have had to work so hard in my career once I became a vet and clearly gone on to be the funniest vet in the world! (I'm sure that's not true.) But I do think I would have enjoyed a lot of aspects of it.

171

And no because I'm not good with blood and guts stuff, studying hurts my brain, I hate taking tests, I don't like working more than twenty minutes a night, I hate responsibility, I'm very sensitive, and I don't think I would take my first cat death well, let alone all the others. In general, I think I would have just gone stir crazy. I like creating. Being a vet to me is maintaining and saving (honorable and amazing work, and I currently do nothing to help anyone and I know that), but I love adding to the world and bringing new ideas and silliness to it. I know enough now as an adult that if I would have become a vet I'd always wonder if I could have become a comic. So now I've split the difference . . . comic that talks about cats too much! The job no one asked me to do but I'm happy to fill in for!

CAT SANCTUARIES AND CAT CAFÉS: A BUCKET LIST FOR A CAT LOVER

A cat sanctuary is a place where cats can live, be taken care of and protected for the rest of their lives. Unlike shelters, they don't try to place animals in homes. Many are open spaces and cats roam free. Free range cats if you will. I LOVE THEM! I love reading about them. I love going to them. I fantasize about being an old lady that runs one. I visited the one in Rome when I was on tour but I wanna go to more.

Cat cafés are kinda a twist on shelters. They are facilities with visiting or play hours with the cats. You make an appointment to come play with cats for a fee (many places treat it like an actual coffee shop and you can get coffee and tea) and all the cats are also up for adoption. So it's a fun way to help the cats have playtime but also for people to spend real time with cats before they decide to adopt them. I love cat cafés!! I've been to them in NYC, Edinburgh, and Los Angeles and my goal is to go to as many as I can. There are sixty-three in the US alone and fourteen in Canada! I have so many trips to plan!

Why Cats are Assholes

My other favorite excursion is just to go to countries with a lot of stray cats. So far the countries I've found to have a lot of stray cats are the Philippines, Thailand, Turkey, and Italy. Many, while they have a lot of strays, have programs that spay/neuter, chip, or tag and release. There are lot of cool programs that have feeding areas and times too. When I was in Manila, Philippines, doing a show the booker saw me stop in my tracks and take pictures of every stray cat I saw and went, "I know where to take you" and took me to this big open area with cats chilling everywhere. He told me they were always there. That's because a group fed them there three times a day and cats know what's up.

Here are a few sanctuaries for your bucket list:

ROME, ITALY

Just a few blocks from the Pantheon is the ancient ruins of Largo Argentina Torre, and among them is the Argentina Cat Sanctuary. It provides a home for around 150 feral cats that roam and sleep in the ruins. Originally fed by locals, in 1994 volunteers took over and began spaying or neutering as many cats as possible to control the population and set up what is now the Argentina Cat Sanctuary.

Volunteers feed and provide care for all stray cats in the city, but the base is still the ruins. It's open to visitors from noon to 6 p.m., and they have a kitty gift shop. You can also donate to them to help feed and take care of the cats.

VET TO THE STRAYS

I told my mom about it when I went a few years ago and she decided right then she was gonna quit her job and move to Rome and be a vet to the Italian strays but immediately learned they were not taking any more vet applications (apparently this is everyone's dream).

SYROS, GREECE

The cat rescue "God's Little People" got a ton of press years ago when an ad for a caretaker went viral. Over forty thousand people applied for the position of caretaker at the sanctuary that houses over seventy cats. If I knew, I would have been one of those applicants! I hope to make it on my next big trip so I can drop off your resume in person :P

AOSHIMA, JAPAN

Japan has ten cat sanctuary islands but the one most talked about is on Aoshima, which used to be an old fishing community and is now nicknamed "Cat Island." There are sixteen people still living on the island and roughly 160 cats. They originally brought them in to control a mice problem. There are day ferries that come so people can visit. My dream is to go here in the next few years!

ACKNOWLEDGMENTS

I wrote a book, guys! This is significant to me cause it's what I went to college for, and who even uses their degree anymore? Are they not just blurs of kinda learning while mostly grappling with parentless freedom that results in an expensive piece of paper and often vague knowledge in something you are starting to think you don't care about? Or was that just me? So thanks to the New School. I learned stuff from you, I used it fifteen years later, and I'm grateful!

Thank you to all my fans that tolerate my Caturday posts. I take an absurd amount of pride in my cat pictures, and it always makes me feel seen when my fans appreciate my cat picture hobby. Additional thanks to all of the fans that participated in my Frequently Asked Cat Questions poll. I used a lot of your questions. Many made me laugh and inspired me to be my silliest, most unhelpful self. Thanks for the support!

Gotta thank my cat, Pasta! Can she read? I don't know, but it doesn't matter. It's like when you post a picture on Instagram of a person who is dead or might as well be dead cause they aren't on Instagram cause they are never gonna see it, but it's the thoughtfulness that other people see that counts. She has been my muse for years, and while she is in the grandma years of her life, I'm grateful for the love, hate, and indifference she has brought to my life for fifteen years.

Also need to thank Pasta's first parents. The Facompre farm: Karen, Rick, and Ashley. Thanks for letting your cats whore it up which resulted in my baby being born. Without your cat's parental negligence, Pasta would have never been. She was from a litter of seven (I believe). And from what I know she has outlived all her siblings and is clearly the most famous. I don't know how I made this about me, but thank you.

Thank you to Barbara Hulick, Kerri Smith, Gwyneth Wyckoff, and everyone at Carnegie Cat Clinic who took care of Pasta when I traveled for work and the two years I traveled too much to be a good cat mom. I'm grateful, and she misses you all. She told me. And special thanks to Kerri for all the beautiful pictures of Pasta, many of which inspired the illustrations in this book.

Mom! Thanks for reading the early version of this and giving your doctor-y notes! Thanks for always laughing at my dumb cat jokes on and off stage and your endless support in everything I do. But also thank you for being the best cat grandma a daughter could ask for. You've provided the best vet care for no money, cured Pasta's cancer, let her room and board for free every time I traveled for work, and eventually let her become a practice cat when my schedule became too much. (I don't have to pay you back now that I'm a super wealthy cat book author, right?) We are literally the definition of the worst clients, yet you only minorly complain about us. We love you and appreciate you. Thanks, Mom.

Dad! I wouldn't be the person or writer I am without your encouragement, excitement, and belief that I can do anything. Everyone knows it's first a long obscure career as a comedian, then a random book about cats no one asked for, then endless fame and money. I'm right on track!

I have so many siblings. They are all the best. Thanks to Emmy for reading my book and for all the Avocado-inspired stories. Theresa for always encouraging my weird career choices and believing in me. Sammy for being my sounding board for weird cat jokes and always one upping me. And Greg for being Greg.

Chelsea Trousdale did all the drawing for the book, and I'm obsessed. I went from fan to super fan. Loved your work before we started and just appreciate how much you encapsulated my stories and ideas. You took this book to the next level. Thank you!

Jason Katzman! (Your name is an inspiration!) This was 100 percent all your doing. Thanks for entrusting me with your brainchild. I'm so happy social media exists and I write too many cat-related jokes so that we could meet. This has been so fun and stressful, but also fun, and I feel so happy to finally have an outlet for all my crazy cat jokes and ideas. Thanks for believing in my voice and for your patience. Sorry for how grammatically awful I am and you knowing to shield me from knowing how much work went into the back side of this. You are magic! I look forward to our next book together, "Why Ferrets Aren't Worth the Effort."

Thanks Irene Branche, my friend, running buddy, free therapist, and all early ideas listener. Amanda Blount, who is my forever cheerleader. Maria Shehata, who makes writing look easy and inspires me every day. Prakash Puru for always telling me I can't do stuff and by that he means he's jealous and wishes he could be me. Michelle Whitcomb, Pasta's early co-parent when

Why Cats are Assholes

I was in college. Carmen Lynch for being Pasta's fairy god-mother. Adrienne Iapalucci and Hari Kondabolu for being my rocks when I needed them. My roommates, Chris Vongsawat and John Crites. The first to hear everything good or bad and just being the best. Isabel Frost for helping make this a reality and understanding its importance. Thanks to Justin Herman for knowing that this meant I'd probably talk about cats more and tolerating it.

And finally: to all ex-boyfriends that were nice to my cat. They say men don't change, but I turned at least a few of them into cat lovers and that feels like it was all worth it.

ABOUT THE AUTHOR

Liz Miele began doing stand-up at age sixteen in New York City, and was profiled in the *New Yorker* magazine two years later. She has appeared on Comedy Central's *Live at Gotham* and *This Week at the Comedy Cellar*, as well as NPR's *Wait Wait Don't Tell Me* and Hulu's *Coming to the Stage*. A native of New Jersey, Miele has toured the world sharing her hilarious stories about life, travel, dating, and, of course, cats. She has three albums you can stream or buy, *Emotionally Exhausting* and *Mind Over Melee*, and her first special, *Self Help Me*, which is also available free on YouTube. She also has a weekly podcast called *2 Non Doctors* with friend and fellow comedian Maria Shehata. Visit www.lizmiele.com for future tour dates and follow on Instagram **@lizmiele** for her Caturday pictures!